W9-AMZ-577

Conversational

GREEK

in 7 Days

*Master Language Survival Skills
in Just One Week!*

Hara Garoufalia-Middle

McGraw·Hill

New York   Chicago   San Francisco   Lisbon   London   Madrid   Mexico City
Milan   New Delhi   San Juan   Seoul   Singapore   Sydney   Toronto

The **McGraw·Hill** Companies

Library of Congress Cataloging-in-Publication Data

Garoufalia-Middle, Hara.
    Conversational Greek in 7 days : master language survival skills in just one
    week! / Hara Garoufalia-Middle.
             p.   cm.
    ISBN 0-07-143276-0 (pkg.) — ISBN 0-07-143275-2 (book)
      1. Greek language, Modern—Conversation and phrase books—English.
  I. Title: Conversational Greek in seven days.   II. Title.

    PA1059.G275   2004
    489′.383421—dc22   2004053146

Originally published by Hodder & Stoughton Publishers.

7 8 9 10 11 12 13 14 15 16 17 18   WKT/WKT   0 9 8 7 6

ISBN 0-07-143276-0 (package)
ISBN 0-07-143275-2 (book)

Acknowledgments
The authors and publishers would like to thank J. Allan Cash Ltd. for the photograph on
page 10, Terry Chisholm for the illustration on page 73, and Barnaby's Library for the
photograph on page 85. All other photographs are reproduced by kind permission of
Howard Middle.

This book is printed on acid-free paper.

CONTENTS

INTRODUCTION

Conversational Greek in 7 Days is a short course that will equip you to deal with everyday situations when you visit Greece and Cyprus: shopping, eating out, asking for directions, changing money, using the phone, and so on.

The course is divided into 7 units, each corresponding to a day in the lives of Anne Johnson, who is staying in Athens, and Peter Hunt, who is on his second trip to the Greek islands. Each unit begins with a dialogue, which introduces the essential language items in context. Key phrases are highlighted in the dialogues, and the phrasebook section that follows lists these and other useful phrases and tells you what they are in English.

Within the units there are also short information sections in English on the topics covered, sections giving basic grammatical explanations, and a number of follow-up activities designed to be useful as well as fun. Answers can be checked in a key at the back of the book. Also available with this program are 2 CDs to help you practice your Greek.

A note about the currency used in this book. In early 2002, 12 countries in the European Union, including Greece, adopted the Euro as the national currency. In this book, the dialogues and text refer to the former currency of Greece, the *drachma*.

BEFORE YOU LEAVE

Introduction to modern Greek

Conversational Greek in 7 Days offers a starter course in modern Greek, and does not attempt to cover Greek grammar comprehensively or in detail. This introduction is to help you understand a few basics about modern Greek grammar. The units that follow will explain everything again, but if you read this first, you'll be better prepared.

Greek nouns, adjectives, and articles ("a" and "the" in English) change their endings according to gender, number, and function in the sentence.

Gender Greek nouns (names of people and things) are divided into three groups: masculine, feminine, neuter. To recognize the gender of the noun, learn the form of the article that goes with it. All nouns in this book will be listed with this article. Some examples:

ο πατέρας   *o pateras*   (the father) – masculine
η μητέρα   *i mitera*   (the mother) – feminine
το παιδί   *to peTHi*   (the child)   – neuter

Once you have learned the typical endings of these three genders, you can guess the gender of any Greek word. French is not so easy!

Number Nouns, and adjectives that qualify them, have two forms: singular for one item; plural for more than one (see page 13).

INTRODUCTION

Function in the sentence Greek nouns have three forms, called cases, indicating: the subject (nominative case); the object (accusative case); possession (genitive case).

The nominative case is used to show the subject of the sentence – the person or thing carrying out an action:

Ο πατέρας θέλει ένα καφέ *o pateras thelei ena kafe* The father wants a coffee

Here, the father is the subject. The article is **o** in the nominative case for a masculine noun. Nominative is also used for the subject of the verb είμαι *ime* (to be).

The accusative case is used to show the object of the sentence – the person or thing to which the action is done, e.g.:

Η Μαρία αγαπάει τον πατέρα *I Maria agapai ton patera* Maria loves the father

Notice how the nominative **o** changes to the accusative "τον" *ton*.

The accusative case always follows prepositions (words of place or direction), e.g.:

από την Κρήτη	*apo tin Kriti*	from Crete
για την Ρόδο	*ya ti Rotho*	for Rhodes
στην Αθήνα	*stin Athina*	in/to Athens

The genitive case is used to show who or what owns something, e.g.:

Το σπίτι του Γιώργου	*to spiti too Yiorgoo*	George's house
Το βιβλίο της Μαρίας	*to vivlio tis Marias*	Maria's book

Articles In Greek the definite article ("the" in English) and the indefinite article ("a" in English) change according to the number, gender, and case of the nouns they define (see Monday, page 12).

Word order Because of the changes to words mentioned above, you can perceive in Greek more clearly the function of words in a sentence. In English you have to rely on word order to tell you who is doing what to whom – compare "Peter loves Anne" with "Anne loves Peter." In Greek, word order is more flexible, as you will discover.

Verbs In Greek, verbs ("doing" words) have endings which change according to the subject, the person or thing doing the action. In English we have to put "I," "you," "we," etc., in front of the verb. In Greek κάνω *kano* means "I make." κάνεις *kaneis* means "you make." The ending is sufficient to show the subject. Of course, Greeks have words for "I," "you," etc., but these are used more for emphasis.

"You" forms Like French, but not like English, Greek has two forms for "you": a "familiar" form for friends, children, relatives; a polite form used for people you don't know, particularly older people or those in authority. This polite form is also the plural of "you," which you'd use for more than one friend or relative.

The familiar form is **εσύ** *esi*. The polite/plural form is **εσείς** *esis*.

The Greek Alphabet

The Greek alphabet has twenty-four letters: seven vowels and seventeen consonants.

Letter		Name	Sound
A	α	alfa	like **a** in r**a**ther
B	β	vita	like **v** in **v**et
Γ	γ	gama	before **a, o, u** sounds, **g** made at the back of the throat; before **e** and **i**, like **y** in **y**et
Δ	δ	THelta	like **th** in **th**at
E	ε	epsilon	like **e** in **e**nvy
Z	ζ	zita	like **z** in **z**ebra
H	η	ita	like **i** in **i**ll
Θ	θ	thita	like **th** in **th**eater
I	ι	iota	before **a** and **o**, like **y** in **y**et; otherwise like **i** in **i**ll
K	κ	kapa	like **k** in **k**ey
Λ	λ	lambda	like **l** in **l**aw
M	μ	mi	like **m** in **m**atch
N	ν	ni	like **n** in **n**ut
Ξ	ξ	ksi	like **x** in mi**x**
O	ο	omikron	like **o** in f**o**g
Π	π	pi	like **p** in **p**et
P	ϱ	ro	like **r** in **r**ed
Σ	σ, ς	sigma	like **s** in **s**oft
T	τ	taf	like **t** in **t**op
Y	υ	ipsilon	like **i** in **i**ll
Φ	φ	fi	like **f** in **f**ire
X	χ	khi	before **e** or **i**, like **h** in **h**and; otherwise pronounce the **h** at the back of your throat
Ψ	ψ	psi	like **ps** in colla**ps**e
Ω	ω	omega	like **o** in **o**live

INTRODUCTION

You will notice that η ita, ι iota, and υ ipsilon, are all pronounced the same. Likewise ο omikron and ω omega.

You will also notice that θ and δ are spelled the same in transliteration, but are pronounced differently. In order to aid pronunciation, you will find that where th is derived from δ it is printed in small capitals – TH – and where it is derived from θ it is in lowercase – th.

ς sigma is used only at the end of words.

Note: only one syllable is normally stressed in a Greek word. This is marked with an acute ´ accent.

Some extra notes on pronunciation

Double vowels (diphthongs) A diphthong consists of two vowels which are pronounced together to make only one sound.

αι	is like e in hen, e.g. , **αίμα** *ema* (blood)
οι	is like ee in meet (but kept short), e.g., **οικογένεια** *ikoyenia* (family)
ει	is also like ee in meet, e.g., **είσοδος** *eesoTHos* (entrance)
αυ	is either af as in **αυτοκίνητο** *aftokinito* (car), or av as in **αυγό** *avgo* (egg)
ευ	is either eff as in **ευχαριστώ** *efharisto* (thank you), or ev as in **Ευρώπη** *evropi* (Europe)
ου	is like oo as in boot, e.g., **μπουζούκι** *boozooki*

Combinations of consonants

μπ	at the beginning of a word is like **b** in **b**ed **μπάρ** *bar* (bar)
μπ	in the middle of a word is like **mb** in la**mb** **γάμπα** *gamba* (leg)
ντ	at the beginning of a word is like **d** in **d**oor **ντούζ** *doos* (shower)
ντ	in the middle of a word is like **nd** as in e**nd** **έντεκα** *endeka* (11)
γκ	at the beginning of a word is like **g** in **g**et **γκάζι** *gazi* (gas)
γκ	in the middle of a word is like **ng** as in sti**ng** **αγκίστρι** *angistri* (hook)
γγ	is like **ng** in so**ng**, e.g., **Άγγλος** *anglos* (only in the middle of a word)
τσ	is like **ts** as in bi**ts**, e.g., **τσιγάρο** *tsigaro* (cigarette)
τζ	is like **tz** as in pi**zz**a, e.g., **τζατζίκι** *tzatziki* (yoghurt and garlic dip)

Note: double consonants are pronounced as if they were single, e.g., **θάλασσα** *thalassa* (sea).

ARRIVING IN GREECE

Hotels are given ratings: Luxury, A, B, C (or Γ gama in Greek). B and C rated hotels will have a breakfast room, but probably not a restaurant. Resort hotels may offer full or more usually half board.

A hotel guide is available ·from the Greek National Tourist Office.

Καλημέρα/Good morning

Anne Johnson is a bank clerk, on her first visit to Athens. She has always been interested in ancient Greece, and has been studying Greek at evening classes.

Anne has arrived at Athens International Airport and she is now looking for a taxi to her hotel.

Anne:	**Καλημέρα.** *kalimera.*
Taxi driver:	Καλημέρα σας. *kalimera sas.*
Anne:	Ξενοδοχείο Ακρόπολη *ksenoτhoheeo akropoli* παρακαλώ. *parakalo.*
Taxi driver:	Μάλιστα κυρία. *malista, kiria.*
Anne:	Εδώ είναι η βαλίτσα μου. *eτho ine i valitsa moo.* **Ευχαριστώ.** *efharisto.*

Words and phrases from the dialogue

Καλημέρα	kalimera	good morning
Ξενοδοχείο	ksenoTHoheeo	hotel
Παρακαλώ	parakalo	please/you're welcome/can I help?*
Μάλιστα	malista	of course/certainly
Κυρία	kiria	madam/Mrs.
Ευχαριστώ	efharisto	thank you
Εδώ είναι	eTHo ine	here is
η βαλίτσα μου	i valitsa moo	my suitcase

*Παρακαλώ *parakalo* means: "please" in a request
"you're welcome" after "thank you"
"can I help you?" in a shop

Other useful phrases

Καλησπέρα	kalispera	good evening
Καληνύχτα	kalinihta	good night
Χαίρετε	herete	hello/goodbye (formal)
Γειά σου/σας	ya soo/sas	hello/goodbye (informal)*
Κύριος	kirios	Mr.
Δεσποινίς	THespinis	Miss
Τι κάνεις/κάνετε	ti kanis/kanete?	How are you?
Καταλαβαίνω	katalaveno	I understand
Δεν καταλαβαίνω	THen katalaveno	I don't understand
Μιλάτε Αγγλικά;	milate anglika?	Do you speak English?

*Γειά σου *ya soo* is used with one person you know well; Γειά σας *ya sas* is used with more than one person, or with one person you don't know.

How to address people in Greek

Mr. Κύριος *kírios* (note the stress on the first syllable)
Mrs. Κυρία *kiría* (second syllable stressed)
Miss Δεσποινίς *THespinís*

Greeks don't yet have a word for "Ms." – when in doubt use κυρία *kiria*.

When you call to someone male, e.g., a waiter, κύριος *kírios* changes its ending to κύριε *kirie*.

Yes and No

Be careful! "Yes" in Greek – **Ναι** *ne* – sounds a bit like "no."

No is Όχι *ohi*. Greeks will often indicate "no" with a combination of raising their eyebrows and making a "tsk" sound.

One of the most useful words in Greek is **Εντάξει** *endaksi* – OK.

FINDING ACCOMMODATIONS

Pensions   Alternatives to hotels, especially on the islands, are "pensions" Πανσιόν *pansion*, or private houses, where rooms Δωμάτια *THOmatia*) can be rented for short periods. There are usually agencies on the harbor front where rooms can be booked, and people soliciting business as each boat comes in. Look for the sign:

ΝΟΙΚΙΑΖΟΥΜΕ ΔΩΜΑΤΙΑ   or just   **ΔΩΜΑΤΙΑ**

Campgrounds are plentiful, and are often advertised by roadside signs miles before their location. A Camping Guide is obtainable from the Greek National Tourist Office (EOT).

Please note   Greek authorities do not allow tourists to sleep on beaches. You will, on arrival, be expected to have some proof of accommodation arrangements.

θέλω ενα δωμάτιο, παρακαλώ
I want a room, please

Peter Hunt is a sales representative, on his second trip to the Greek islands. He's crazy about all kinds of water sports and night life!

Peter has just gotten off the boat from Piraeus, and is now looking for somewhere to stay on the beautiful island of Paros. He hasn't bothered to book in advance. Typical!

Travel agent:	Δωμάτια, δωμάτια! Rooms, rooms!
	тнomatia, тнomatia! rooms, rooms!
Peter:	**Θέλω ένα δωμάτιο, παρακαλώ.**
	тнelo ena тнomatio, parakalo.
Travel agent:	Για πόσες μέρες;
	ya posses meres?
Peter:	Για πέντε μέρες. Έχετε;
	ya pende meres. ehete?
Travel agent:	Ναι, βεβαίως κύριε. Έχω ένα πολύ ωραίο κοντά στη
	ne, veveos, kirie. eho ena poli oreo, konda sti
	θάλασσα.
	thalassa.
Peter:	**Πόσο κάνει;**
	posso kani?
Travel agent:	Το δωμάτιο είναι πολύ φτηνό. Μόνο δύο χιλιάδες
	to тнomatio ine poli ftino. mono тнio hiliaтнes
	δραχμές με ντουζ.
	тнrahmes, me doos.
Peter:	Εντάξει. Ευχαριστώ.
	endaksi. efharisto.

Words and phrases from the dialogue

Θέλω ένα δωμάτιο	*thelo ena THomatio*	I want a room
Για πόσες μέρες;	*ya posses meres?*	for how many days?
Για πέντε μέρες	*ya pende meres*	for five days
Έχετε;	*ehete?*	Do you have (any)?
Βεβαίως	*veveos*	of course
Έχω ένα πολύ ωραίο	*eho ena poli oreo*	I have a very nice one
Κοντά στη θάλασσα	*konda sti THalassa*	near the sea
Πόσο κάνει;	*posso kani?*	How much?
Πολύ φτηνό	*poli ftino*	very cheap
Μόνο δύο χιλιάδες δραχμές	*mono THio hiliaTHes THrahmes*	only 2000 drachmas
Με ντους	*me doos*	with a shower

Other useful phrases

Σήμερα	*simera*	today
Χθές	*hthes*	yesterday
αύριο	*avrio*	tomorrow
(η) μέρα	*(i) mera*	day
(η) νύχτα	*(i) nihta*	night (after midnight)
(το) πρωί	*(to) proee*	early morning
(το) βράδυ	*(to) vraTHee*	evening (7:00 to 12:00 pm)
(το) απόγευμα	*(to) apoyevma*	afternoon (3:00 to 7:00 pm)
(το) μεσημέρι	*(to) mesimeri*	noon (between 12 noon and 3)

The siesta Especially in the hot summer months, Greek people have several hours of rest after lunch – between 2:00 pm and 5:30 pm – before going back to work for the evening period. People try not to make too much noise, or play their stereos loud during this time. After 5:30, though, life gets going again.

the way it works

Definite article

You saw in the dialogue the word for "the" **το** *to*, used with the word **δωμάτιο** *THomatio* (room). **Δωμάτιο** *THomatio* is a neuter noun.

With a feminine noun, e.g., **βαλίτσα** *valitsa* (suitcase), the definite article form is **η** *(i)*, as in η βαλίτσα.

With a masculine noun, the article is **ο** *(o)* e.g., ο **όροφος,** o orofos (floor of a house/hotel) – see the dialogue on page 14.

Indefinite article

The equivalent forms for the indefinite article ("a" in English) are:

masculine:	ἕνας	enas	ἕνας κύριος	enas kirios a man
feminine:	μία	mia	μία κυρία	mia kiria a lady
neuter:	ἕνα	ena	ἕνα παιδί	ena peTHi a child

These are the nominative forms (see Introduction) – you'll see later how these forms change according to the function (case) of the noun in the sentence.

Plural Note that δωμάτιο THomatio becomes δωμάτια THomatia in the plural. Η μέρα I mera (the day) becomes μέρες meres, in Για πόσες μέρες ya posses meres. These are typical ways neuter and feminine nouns change in the plural (see page 33 for a full list of plural forms).

Note: In this book all nouns listed are given in the nominative case, i.e., the case used with the subject of the sentence.

Possessive adjectives

Note that the definite article comes before the noun, and the possessive adjective comes after.

The Greek word for "my" (possessive adjective) is μου moo.

Η βαλίτσα μου   i valitsa moo   my suitcase

Unlike French or German, where the "my" form changes with gender and number, in Greek the form is constant – a lot easier!

The possessive adjectives are:

μου	moo	my		μας	mas	our
σου	soo	your (sing./fam.)		σας	sas	your (pl./polite)
του	too	his		τους	toos	their (masc.)
της	tis	her		τους	toos	their (fem.)
του	too	its		τους	toos	their (neut.)

e.g.:

Το δωμάτιό σας είναι το εκατόν είκοσι your room is number 120
to THomatio sas ine to ekaton ikosi
Το διαβατήριό μου είναι εδώ   my passport is here
to THiavatirio moo ine eTHO
Το τσάι μας είναι κρύο   our tea is cold
to tsai mas ine krio

things to do

1.1 Practice greeting the following people at different times of the day:

1   Mrs. Pavlou, hotel manager (say good morning)
2   Mr. Stavropoulos, a business contact (say good evening)
3   Maria, a friend (say a friendly hello)
4   Miss Niarchou (say a formal hello)

AT THE HOTEL

Ένα μονόκλινο, με μπάνιο
A single room with bath

Anne Johnson arrives at her hotel, where, unlike Peter, she has reserved a room in advance.

Hotel clerk: Παρακαλώ;
parakalo?

Anne: **Το όνομά μου είναι** Johnson. **Ορίστε το διαβατήριό μου.**
to onoma mou ine Johnson. oriste to THiavatirio mou.

Clerk: Α! ναι, κυρία Johnson. Το δωμάτιό σας είναι έτοιμο.
ah, ne, Kiria Johnson. to THomatio sas ine etimo.
Ένα μονόκλινο, με μπάνιο.
Ena monoklino, me banyo.

Anne: Πολύ καλά, ευχαριστώ. Τι όροφος παρακαλώ;
poli kala, efharisto. ti orofos, parakalo?

Clerk: Το δωμάτιό σας είναι το εκατόν είκοσι, στον πρώτο όροφο.
to THomatio sas ine to ekaton ikosi, ston proto orofo.

Anne: Εντάξει. **Τι ώρα έχει πρωινό;**
endaksi. ti ora ehi proino?

Clerk: Από τις επτά μέχρι τις δέκα. Εδώ είναι το κλειδί σας.
apo tis epta, mehri tis THeka. eTHo ine to kleeTHi sas.
Καλώς ορίσατε!
kalos orisate!

Words and phrases from the dialogue

Το όνομά μου είναι	*to onoma mou ine*	my name is . . .
Ορίστε	*oriste*	here it is
Το διαβατήριό μου	*to thiavatirio moo*	my passport
Το δωμάτιό σας είναι **έτοιμο**	*to thomatio sas ine* *etimo*	your room is ready
Ένα μονόκλινο, **με μπάνιο**	*ena monoklino,* *me banyo*	a single, with bath

Πολύ καλά	poli kala	very good/fine
Τι όροφος;	ti orofos?	Which floor?
Το εκατόν είκοσι	to ekaton ikosi	number 120
Στον πρώτο όροφο	ston proto orofo	on the first floor
Τι ώρα;	ti ora . . . ?	What time . . . ?
Το πρωινό	to proino	breakfast
Από τις...μέχρι τις...	apo tis . . . mehri tis . . .	from . . . to . . .
Το κλειδί σας	to kleeΤΗi sas	your key
Καλώς ωρίσατε!	kalos orisate!	Welcome!

Numbers 0–22

0	μηδέν	miΤΗen	11	έντεκα	enΤΗeka
1	ένα/μία	ena/mia	12	δώδεκα	thoΤΗeka
2	δύο	ΤΗio	13	δεκατρία	ΤΗekatria
3	τρία/τρείς	tria/tris	14	δεκατέσσερα	ΤΗekatessera
4	τέσσερα	tessera	15	δεκαπέντε	ΤΗekapende
	τέσσερις	tesseris	16	δεκαέξι	ΤΗekaeksi
5	πέντε	pende	17	δεκαεπτά	ΤΗekaepta
6	έξι	eksi	18	δεκαοκτώ	ΤΗekaokto
7	εφτά/επτά	efta/epta	19	δεκαεννέα	ΤΗekaenea
8	οκτώ/οχτώ	okto/ohto	20	είκοσι	ikosi
9	εννέα/εννιά	enea/ennia	21	είκοσι ένα	ikosi ena
10	δέκα	ΤΗeka	22	είκοσι δύο	ikosi ΤΗio

1st	πρώτος	protos	7th	έβδομος	evΤΗomos
2nd	δεύτερος	ΤΗefteros	8th	όγδοος	ogΤΗoos
3rd	τρίτος	tritos	9th	ένατος	enatos
4th	τέταρτος	tetartos	10th	δέκατος	ΤΗekatos
5th	πέμπτος	pemptos	11th	ενδέκατος	enΤΗekatos
6th	έκτος	ektos			

Other useful phrases

Έχω κλείσει	eho kleesee	I've reserved
Έχετε δωμάτια;	ehete ΤΗomatia?	Do you have any rooms?
Μπορώ να το δώ;	boro na to ΤΗo?	Can I see it?
(Ένα) μονόκλινο	(ena) monoklino	a single room
(Ένα) δίκλινο	(ena) diklino	a double room
(Ένα) τρίκλινο	(ena) triklino	a 3-bed room
Με διπλό κρεβάτι	me ΤΗiplo krevati	with a double bed
Με δύο κρεβάτια	me ΤΗio krevatya	with two beds
Υπογράψτε	ipograpste	sign (please)
Δεν έχουμε	ΤΗen ehoume	We don't have (any)
Είμαστε γεμάτοι	imaste yemati	We're full
Η τουαλέτα	i tooaleta	toilet
Η πετσέτα	i petseta	towel
Το σαπούνι	to sapooni	soap
Το χαρτί τουαλέτας	to harti tooaletas	toilet paper
Ο λογαριασμός	o logariasmos	bill

the way it works

Neuter nouns

Neuter nouns can be recognized by their endings ο, η, μα, e.g.:

το δωμάτιο	*to THomatio*	the room
το διαβατήριο	*to THiavatirio*	the passport
το κλειδί	*to kleeTHi*	the key
το όνομα	*to onoma*	the name

(see page 33 for masculine and feminine forms)

Adjectives

Adjectives in Greek have to agree with the noun they qualify, e.g.:

Το δωμάτιο είναι έτοιμο   *to THomatio ine etimo*   the room is ready

Verbs

You have met three important verbs so far:

Θέλω   *thelo*   I want   **έχω**   *eho*   I have   **είμαι**   *ime*   I am

When you talk about a verb in Greek you use the "I" form, as there is no infinitive (to have).

This is how a regular Greek verb is conjugated:

θέλω	*thelo*	I want	**θέλουμε**	*theloome*	we want
θέλεις	*thelis*	you want (sing.)	**θέλετε**	*thelete*	you want (plur.)
θέλει	*theli*	he/she/it wants	**θέλουν(ε)**	*theloon(e)*	they want

eho (I have) has the same endings:

έχω	*eho*	I have	**έχουμε**	*ehoome*	we have
έχεις	*ehis*	you have (sing.)	**έχετε**	*ehete*	you have (plur.)
έχει	*ehi*	he/she/it has	**έχουν(ε)**	*ehoon(e)*	they have

However, ime (I am) is irregular:

Είμαι	*ime*	I am	**Είμαστε**	*imaste*	we are
Είσαι	*eise*	you are (sing.)	**Είστε/είσαστε**	*iste/isaste*	you are (plur.)
Είναι	*ine*	he/she/it is	**Είναι**	*ine*	they are

Note: The polite form of "you": you normally use the second person *plural* form of the verb when talking to someone you don't know well.

Negative/Interrogative

The negative is easy in Greek – just put δεν, pronounced "then," in front of the verb:

Δεν έχουμε δωμάτια *THen ehoome THomatia* – we don't have any rooms.

To ask a question only the intonation changes, not the word order, as in English. Listen again, if you have the cassette.

Personal pronouns

In the Introduction we noted that Greeks do not use personal pronouns as much as in English, because the endings of the verbs themselves give the person. Greek personal pronouns are:

Εγώ	*ego*	I	**Εμείς**	*emis*	we
Εσύ	*esi*	you (sing. fam. form)	**Εσείς**	*esis*	you (plural, formal)
Αυτός	*aftos*	he	**Αυτοί**	*afti*	they (m.)
Αυτή	*afti*	she	**Αυτές**	*aftes*	they (f.)
Αυτό	*afto*	it	**Αυτά**	*afta*	they (n.)

Τσάϊ με λεμόνι, παρακαλώ
Tea with lemon, please

In the hotel restaurant, Anne decides to have a late breakfast.

Waiter: Καλημέρα κυρία. Τσάι ή καφέ;
Kalimera kiria. tsai i kafe?

Anne: **Τσάι με λεμόνι παρακαλώ.**
tsai me lemoni parakalo.

Waiter: Θέλετε αυγά με μπέικον;
thelete avga me beicon?

Anne: **Όχι ευχαριστώ.** Μόνο τοστ, με βούτηρο και μαρμελάδα.
ohi efharisto. mono tost, me vootiro ke marmelaτha.

Waiter: Μάλιστα. **Ο αριθμός του δωματίου σας;**
malista. o arithmos too τhomatioo sas?

Anne: Εκατόν είκοσι.
ekaton ikosi.

Words and phrases from the dialogue

τσάι ή καφέ	tsai i kafe	tea or coffee
με λεμόνι	me lemoni	with lemon
αυγά με μπέικον	avga me beicon	eggs and bacon
μόνο τοστ	mono tost	only toast
το βούτυρο	to vootiro	butter
η μαρμελάδα	i marmelaTHa	jam/marmalade
ο αριθμός	o arithmos	number
του δωματίου σας	too THomatioo sas	of your room
εκατόν είκοσι	ekaton ikosi	120

Other useful phrases

το πρωινό	to proino	breakfast
το μεσημεριανό	to mesimeriano	lunch
το βραδυνό	to vraTHino	dinner
το γάλα	to gala	milk
χυμός πορτοκάλι	himos portokali	orange juice
καφέ με γάλα	kafe me gala	coffee with milk
χωρίς γάλα	horis gala	without milk
ακόμα λίγο καφέ,	akoma ligo kafe,	more coffee,
παρακαλώ	parakalo	please
το αλάτι	to alati	salt
το πιπέρι	to piperi	pepper
ζεστό νερό	zesto nero	hot water
βραστό αυγό	vrasto avgo	boiled egg
τηγανητό αυγό	tiganito avgo	fried egg
η ζάχαρη	i zahari	sugar
το ψωμί	to psomi	bread
το μαχαίρι	to maheri	knife
το πιρούνι	to pirooni	fork
το κουτάλι	to kootali	spoon

things to do

1.2 Practice reserving different sorts of room at a hotel. Use θέλω *thelo* (I want/I would like).

1

2

3

4

5

1.3 You have arrived at a hotel where you have a reservation. Can you fill in your part of the conversation with the receptionist?

You:	(say good morning)
Receptionist:	Το όνομά σας παρακαλώ;
	to onoma sas, parakalo?
You:	(give your name)
Receptionist:	Ναι, ένα δίκλινο, με ντους. Το διαβατήριό σας;
	ne, ena THiklino, me doos. to THiavatirio sas?
You:	(offer your passport)
Receptionist:	Υπογράψτε εδώ παρακαλώ
	ipograpste eTHo, parakalo
You:	(ask what time breakfast is served)

1.4 Practice saying these room numbers:

1 [3]   2 [12]   3 [17]

4 [10]   5 [14]

1.5 Order breakfast for the following people using θέλω *thelo* with the right form of the verb:

1 yourself (I) (tea with milk, eggs, and bacon)
2 your son (he) (coffee, toast, and jam)
3 all of you (we) (orange juice)
4 your daughter (she) (tea with lemon, toast, boiled egg)

FINDING YOUR WAY AROUND

Museums   There are many museums in Athens, and nearby famous archeological sites. The two not to miss in Athens are the National Archeological Museum, and the new Acropolis Museum on the site of the Parthenon.

It's a good idea to get a guidebook and read up a little on ancient Greek history before you arrive.

Check regulations about photography – some museums allow you to take photographs as long as you don't use a flash. Others have a charge for flash photography.

Που είναι η Ακρόπολις;
Where is the Acropolis?

Anne is checking her map of Athens. She asks the hotel receptionist for some help in getting to the Acropolis.

Anne: **Συγνώμη, που είναι η** Ακρόπολι; (showing her map)
         signomi, poo ine I Acropoli?

Receptionist: Είμαστε εδώ στο χάρτη στη γωνία. Η Ακρόπολις είναι εκεί.
         imaste ετηο sto harti sti gonia. I Acropolis ine eki.
         Στρίψτε δεξιά από την πόρτα μας, και πάρτε το
         stripste ΤΗeksia apo tin porta mas, ke parte to
         δεύτερο δρόμο αριστερά.
         ΤΗeftero ΤΗromo aristera.

Anne: **Είναι μακριά με τα πόδια;**
         ine makria me ta ροτΗia?

Receptionist: Όχι το πολύ δέκα λεπτά.
         ohi, to poli ΤΗeka lepta.

Anne: Ευχαριστώ. Η αρχαία Ελλάδα με περιμένει!
         efharisto. i arhea ellaΤΗa me perimeni!

Words and phrases from the dialogue

Συγνώμη	*signomi*	Excuse me, sorry
Που είναι;	*poo ine?*	Where is/are . . . ?
εδώ	*eTHO*	here
ο χάρτης	*o hartis*	map
στον χάρτη	*ston harti*	on the map
εκεί	*eki*	there
στη γωνία	*sti gonia*	at the corner
στρίψτε δεξιά	*stripste THeksia*	turn right*
αριστερά	*aristera*	left
από την πόρτα μας	*apo tin porta mas*	from our door/entrance
πάρτε το δεύτερο δρόμο	*parte to THeftero THromo*	take the 2nd street . . .
μακριά/κοντά	*makria/konda*	far/near
με τα πόδια	*me ta pothia*	on foot
το πολύ	*to poli*	at the most
δέκα λεπτά	*THeka lepta*	ten minutes
Η αρχαία Ελλάδα με περιμένει	*i arhea ellaTHa me perimeni*	Ancient Greece awaits me!

* See page 38 for imperatives (giving orders).

Other useful words and phrases

η οδός	*i OTHOS*	road/street (used in names/formal)
ο δρόμος	*o THromos*	road/street
το στενό	*to steno*	side street
η λεωφόρος	*i leoforos*	avenue
η πλατεία	*i platia*	square
το κέντρο	*to kendro*	center
η στάση	*i stasi*	(bus) stop
απέναντι	*apenandi*	opposite
μετά ευθεία	*meta efthia*	afterwards straight ahead
στην οδό...	*stin OTHO . . .*	into . . . road/street

Που είναι το τουριστικό γραφείο;
poo ine to tooristiko grafio?   Where is the tourist office?

Έχετε το χάρτη της πόλης;
ehete to harti tis polis?   Do you have a map of the town?

Υπάρχει τράπεζα εδώ κοντά;
iparhi trapeza eTHO konda?   Is there a bank near here?

Πιο σιγά παρακαλώ, δεν καταλαβαίνω.
pyo siga parakalo, THen katalaveno.   Slower, please, I don't understand .

Πέστε το ξανά, παρακαλώ.
peste to ksana, parakalo.   Say that again, please.

| ανοικτό | *anikto* | open | κλειστό | *klisto* | closed |

MEETING PEOPLE

Απο που είστε;/Where are you from?

Anne is walking to the Acropolis and sees a couple ahead of her. She wants to check whether she is on the right road.

Anne: **Συγνώμη, αυτός είναι ο δρόμος για την Ακρόπολη;**
signomi, aftos ine o THromos ya tin akropoli?

Man: Ναι δεσποινίς. Ελάτε μαζί μας. Και εμείς πηγαίνουμε εκεί.
ne, THespinis. elate mazi mas. ke emis piyenoome eki.

Woman: Από που είστε;
apo poo iste?

Anne: **Είμαι από την Αγγλία.**
ime apo tin anglia.

Man: Πόσο καιρό είστε στην Αθήνα;
posso kero iste stin athina?

Anne: Μόνο μία μέρα, **είναι η πρώτη επίσκεψή μου στην Ελλάδα.**
Mono mia mera, ine i proti episkepsi moo stin ellaτHa.

As they walk up the steps to the Acropolis, Yiannis Vazakas introduces himself.

Yiannis: **Με λένε** Γιάννη Βαζάκα, (pointing to his wife)
me lene yanni vazaka.
Η γυναίκα μου Ελένη.
i yineka moo, eleni.

Anne: **Χαίρω πολύ**. Με λένε Anne Johnson.
hero poli. me lene Anne Johnson.
Αγαπάω πολύ την ιστορία της Ελλάδας.
Agapao poli tin istoria tis Ellaτhas.

Yiannis: Αλήθεια; Εγώ είμαι αρχαιολόγος.
Alithea? Ego ime arheologos.

Words and phrases from the dialogue

ο δρόμος για	o THromos ya	the road/street to . . .
ελάτε μαζί μας	elate mazi mas	come with us
Από που είστε;	apo poo iste?	Where are you from?
Είμαι από την Αγγλία.	ime apo tin anglia.	I'm from England.
η Αγγλία	i anglia	England
η Ελλάδα	i ellaTHa	Greece
Πόσο καιρό είστε στην Ελλάδα;	posso kero iste stin ellaTHa?	How long have you been in Greece?
μία μέρα	mia mera	one day
η πρώτη επίσκεψή μου στην Ελλάδα;	i proti episkepsi moo stin ellaTHa	my first visit in/to Greece
με λένε	me lene	my name is/I'm called
η γυναίκα μου	i yineka moo	my wife
Χαίρω πολύ	hero poli	How do you do?
Είμαι αρχαιολόγος.	ime arheologos.	I'm an archeologist.

Making conversation

Τι δουλεία κάνετε;	ti THoolia kanete?	What's your job? (= what work do you do?) see p. 94
Είμαι/είμαστε εδώ για διακοπές.	ime/imaste eTHo ya thiakopes.	I'm/we're here on vacation.
Είμαι εδώ για δουλειά	ime eTHo ya THoolia.	I'm here on business.
Είστε μόνος/μόνη σας;	iste monos/moni sas?	Are you on your own?
Είμαι με τη γυναίκα μου.	ime me ti yineka moo	I'm with my wife.
τον άντρα μου	ton andra moo	my husband.
την οικογένειά μου	tin ikoyenia moo	my family.
μερικούς φίλους	merikoos filoos	some friends.
Είμαι φοιτητής/φοιτήτρια.	ime fititis/fititria	I'm a student (m/f).
Τι σπουδάζετε;	ti spooTHazete?	What do you study?
Σπουδάζω ιατρική.	spooTHazo iatriki.	I'm studying medicine.
Είμαι Άγγλος.	ime Anglos.	I'm English (masc.).
Είμαι Αγγλίδα.	ime AngliTHa.	I'm English (fem.).

the way it works

Accusative case

As you saw in the Introduction, the word that is the object of a sentence is put into the accusative case in Greek. The ending of the word can change, depending on the gender, as well as the article that precedes it.

Singular

ο άνθρωπος	*o anthropos*	becomes	τον άνθρωπο/ *ton anthropo*
η μητέρα	*i mitera*	becomes	την μητέρα/ *tin mitera*
το παιδί	*to peτHi*	remains the same in the accusative	

Plural

οι άνθρωποι	*i anthropi*	becomes	τους ανθρώπους/ *toos anthropoos*
οι μητέρες	*i miteres*	becomes	τις μητέρες/ *tis miteres*
τα παιδιά	*ta peτHia*	remains the same in the accusative	

Prepositions

After prepositions (e.g., in, at, on) we use the accusative case.

Common Greek prepositions are

σε	*se*	in/at/to
από	*apo*	from/out of
για	*ya*	for
με	*me*	with
μαζί	*mazi*	together
μέχρι	*mehri*	until
χωρίς	*horis*	without
πριν	*prin*	before
μετά	*meta*	after

Σε se combines with the definite article in the accusative case to produce **στη(ν)** stin (fem.), **στο(ν)** sto(n) (masc.), **στο** sto (neut.), e.g.:

στη γωνία	*sti gonia*	at the corner
στον πρώτο όροφο	*ston proto orofo*	on the first floor
στο πάρκο	*sto parko*	in the park

Agreement of adjectives

Adjectives always agree with the noun they qualify in terms of gender, number, and case. In the dialogue Anne says **Η αρχαία Ελλάδα με περιμένει** *i arhea ellaτHa me perimeni*. As Ελλάδα *ellaτHa* (Greece) is feminine, the adjective αρχαία *arhea* (ancient) is also feminine.

With a masculine noun the same adjective would have the masculine ending **-ος** *-os*, e.g., **ο αρχαίος ναός** *o arheos naos* (the ancient temple).

With a neuter noun the ending **-ο** *-o* is used, e.g., **το αρχαίο κτίριο** *to arheo ktirio* (the ancient building). Το τουριστικό γραφείο *To touristiko grafio* (tourist office).

Note: the ending for the feminine adjective is either **-α** *-a* or **-η** *-i*, e.g.:

ωραία	*orea*	nice	μικρή	*mikri*	small

The genitive case

In the Introduction, the function of the genitive case was explained – to show ownership.

In the dialogue on page 17 you saw:

Ο αριθμός του δωματίου σας   the number of your room
o arithmos too THomatioo sas

το δωμάτιο   *to THomatio* (nominative case) becomes
του δωματίου   *too THomatioo* (genitive case).

In the dialogue on page 23 you saw:

Αγαπάω πολύ την ιστορία της Ελλάδας   I love the history of Greece very much
agapao poli tin istoria tis ellaTHas

Some more examples:

"John's key" in Greek
  would be   Το κλειδί του Γιάννη   *to kliTHi too Yanni*
"Mary's passport"   Το διαβατήριο της Μαρίας *to THiavatirio tis Marias*
"The child's toy"   Το παιχνίδι του παιδιού   *to pehniTHi too peTHioo*

things to do

2.1   **Making conversation**   You've met a very inquisitive Greek person, who wants to know all about you!

Greek: Από που είστε;
You: (from England)
Greek: Τι δουλειά κάνετε;
You: (say what you do – see list page 94)
Greek: Είστε εδώ με την οικογένειά σας;
You: (yes, with your wife/husband/some friends)
Greek: Πόσο καιρό είστε στην Ελλάδα;
You: (three days)
Greek: Που μένετε;
You: (at the Hotel Acropolis)

PUBLIC TRANSPORTATION

Air Athens' new airport, Eleftherios Venizelos, is about 27 km (17 mi) from Athens. There is convenient bus service from the airport to downtown Athens.

Bus Greece has an excellent service of long-distance buses. Public buses within cities are an inexpensive way to get around. In larger cities, you can purchase bus tickets at a kiosk, but in smaller cities, fares often are paid on board.

Trolley Athens has cheap and frequent trolley service. You should purchase your ticket at a kiosk before boarding and validate it using one of the machines on board.

Subway The Metro in Athens consists of three different lines: an older line that was constructed in the 19th century and runs to the harbor of Pireaus, as well as two recently constructed lines that criss-cross central Athens.

Electric train   The partially underground electric train service
(**ο ηλεκτρικός** *ilektrikos*) is a single line running north–south
through Athens from Kifisya to Piraeus, via Omonia Square.

Taxis   No visit to Athens is complete without an exhilarating
drive in a Greek taxi! They are cheap, and there's no need to tip,
just round up to the nearest ten drachmas. Look for the sign
ΕΛΕΥΘΕΡΟ *elefthero* in the driver's window; if it is raised, the
taxi is free. At night, the taxi sign stays lit, even if the taxi is
occupied. Taxis will often take on several separate passengers en
route if they're going in the same direction. There are some radio
taxis in Athens now.

In Athens during weekdays there can be traffic restrictions to
reduce exhaust pollution, which affect taxis. Taxis with even
registration numbers can circulate only in the inner ring
(**δακτύλιος** *THaktilios*) on even number dates, and vice-versa. Thus
you'll see next to the taxi sign on the roof of the car either the
letter *Z* or *M.* These means:

Ζυγός   *zigos*   even
Μονός   *monos*   odd

If you want to travel in the center of town, therefore, make sure
you know which taxi to hail!

Πηγαίνει αυτό το λεωφορείο στην πλάζ;
Does this bus go to the beach?

Peter decides to take the bus to go to the beach.

Peter: Συγνώμη, **πηγαίνει αυτό το λεωφορείο στην πλαζ;**
signomi, piyeni afto to leoforio stin plaz?

Driver: Ναι, φεύγει σε δέκα λεπτά.
ne, fevyi se THeka lepta.

Peter: **Πόσο κάνει το εισιτήριο;**
posso kani to isitirio?

Driver: Ογδόντα δραχμές.
ogTHonda THrahmes.

Peter: **Σε ποιά στάση θα κατεβώ;**
se pya stasi tha katevo?

Driver: **Στη Χρυσή Άμμο – θα σας πω.**
sti hrisi amo – tha sas po.

Words and phrases from the dialogue

Πηγαίνει αυτό το λεωφορείο	piyeni afto to leoforio	Does this bus go . . . ?
στην πλαζ	stin plaz	to the beach
φεύγει	fevyi	it leaves
σε δέκα λεπτά	se THeka lepta	in ten minutes
πόσο κάνει	posso kani	How much is . . . ?*
το εισητήριο	to isitirio	the ticket
ογδόντα δραχμές	ogTHonda THrahmes	80 drachmas (see p. 31)
σε ποιά στάση	se pya stasi	(at) which stop . . . ?
θα κατέβω	tha katevo	I'll get off
θα σας πω	tha sas po	I'll tell you
Στη Χρυσή Άμμο	sti hrisi amo	at "Golden Sand"

*To say "How much are . . . ?", the phrase changes to:
πόσο κάνουν; *posso kanoon?*

Travel and transportation signs

ΑΦΙΞΕΙΣ	afiksis	arrivals
ΑΝΑΧΩΡΗΣΕΙΣ	anahorisis	departures
ΠΛΗΡΟΦΟΡΕΙΕΣ	plirofories	information
ΤΕΛΩΝΕΙΟ	telonio	customs
ΕΛΕΓΧΟΣ	elenhos	passport
ΔΙΑΒΑΤΗΡΙΟΝ	THiavatirion	control
ΕΙΣΟΔΟΣ	isoTHos	entrance
ΕΞΟΔΟΣ	eksoTHos	exit

Other useful words and phrases

Τι ώρα έχει λεωφορείο/τρένο/πούλμαν/αεροπλάνο/πλοίο για *ti ora ehi leoforio/treno/pulman/aeroplano/plio ya . . .*	What time is there a bus, train, coach, plane, boat to . . . ?
Τι ώρα/Πότε είναι το επόμενο/τελευταίο λεωφορείο για *ti ora/pote ine to epomeno/telefteo leoforio ya . . .*	What time is the next/last bus to . . . ?
Που μπορώ να πάρω ενα λεωφορείο για . . . *poo boro na paro ena leoforio ya . . .*	Where can I get a bus to . . . ?
Το λεωφορείο είναι γεμάτο. *to leoforio ine yemato.*	The bus is full.
Πόση ώρα κάνει το λεωφορείο για . . . *posi ora kani to leoforio ya . . .*	How long does the bus take to . . . ?
Είναι ελεύθερη (αυτή η θέση); *ine eleftheri (afti i thesi)?*	Is this seat free?
Πρέπει να αλλάξω (λεωφορείο); *prepi na alakso (leoforio)?*	Do I have to change (buses)?
Είναι το τραίνο στην ώρα του; *ine to treno stin ora too?*	Is the train on time?
Το αεροπλάνο έχει καθυστέρηση. *to aeroplano ehi kathisterisi.*	The plane is delayed.

Greek money

The drachma δραχμή THrahmi is the name of the currency.
COINS: 1, 2, 5, 10, 20, 50 (new coin) drachmas δραχμές
BILLS: 50 (being phased out), 100, 500, 1000, 5000 drachmas

Numbers and money

30	τριάντα	trianda	100	εκατό(ν)	ekato(n)	(drachmas)
40	σαράντα	saranda	200	διακόσια	THiakosia	-es
50	πενήντα	peninda	300	τριακόσια	triakosia	-es
60	εξήντα	eksinda	400	τετρακόσια	tetrakosia	-es
70	εβδομήντα	evTHominda	500	πεντακόσια	pendakosia	-es
80	ογδόντα	ogthonda	600	εξακόσια	eksakosia	-es
90	ενενήντα	eneninda	700	εφτακόσια	eftakosia	-es
			800	οχτακόσια	oktakosia	-es
			900	εννιακόσια	enyakosia	-es

1000	χίλια	hilia
	χίλιες	hilies (fem. for drachmas)
2000	δύο χιλιάδες	THio hiliaTHes
3000	τρεις χιλιάδες	tris hiliaTHes
4000	τέσσερις χιλιάδες	tesseris hiliaTHes

105	εκατόν πέντε	ekaton pende
124	εκατόν είκοσι τέσσερα	ekaton ikosi tessera

1675   χίλια εξακόσια εβδομήντα πέντε
hilia eksakosia evTHominda pende
χίλιες εξακόσιες εβδομήντα πέντε δραχμές
hilies eksakosies evTHominda pende THrahmes

the way it works

Telling the time

Some basic words and phrases (see pages 15 and 31 for numbers):

η ώρα	*i ora*	hour
το λεπτό	*to lepto*	minute (plural τα λεπτά *ta lepta*)
τι ώρα είναι;	*ti ora ine?*	What time is it?
και τέταρτο	*ke tetarto*	quarter past
παρά τέταρτο	*para tetarto*	quarter to
και μισή	*ke misi*	half past
σε πέντε λεπτά	*se pende lepta*	in 5 minutes

Η ώρα είναι μία/δύο/τρείς/τέσσερις.	It's 1/2/3/4 o'clock.
i ora ine mia/THio/tris/tesseris.	
στις μία/δύο/τρεις/τέσσερις.	at 1/2/3/4 o'clock.
stis mia/THio/tris/tesseris	
Είναι πέντε και τέταρτο/μισή.	It's a quarter/half past five.
ine pende ke tetarto/misi.	
στις πέντε παρά τέταρτο	at a quarter to five
stis pende para tetarto	

You may hear alternatives for half past the hour:

μιάμιση	*miamisi*	1:30
δυόμιση	*thiomisi*	2:30
τρεισήμιση	*trisimisi*	3:30
τεσσερισήμιση	*teserisimisi*	4:30
πεντέμιση	*pendemisi*	5:30

Note that the hour always comes first, and the minutes follow.

τρείς παρά είκοσι πέντε	*tris para ikosi pende*	
or		} 2:35/twenty-five to three
δύο και τριάντα πέντε	*THio ke trianda pende*	

π.μ.(προ μεσημβρίας)	*pro mesimvrias*	am
μ.μ. (μετά μεσημβρίας)	*meta mesimvrias*	pm

This and that

The words for "this" and "that" in Greek are αυτός *aftos* this and εκείνος *ekinos* that. These are adjectives and have to agree in number, case, and gender with the noun to which they refer, e.g.:

αυτός ο δρόμος	*aftos o THromos*	this road
εκείνη η εκκλησία	*ekini i eklisia*	that church

Notice that you must use the definite article as well; literally you say "this the road."

Which? and Who?

The word for which?/who? in Greek is

ποιός	pyos	(masc.)
ποιά	pya	(fem.)
ποιό	pyo	(neut.)

Like **αυτός/εκείνος** *aftos/ekinos* these are also adjectives and have to agree with the noun to which they refer, e.g.:

Ποιό λεωφορείο πάει στην Ακρόπολη; Which bus goes to the Acropolis?
pyo leoforio pai stin akropoli?
Ποιός είναι ο κύριος Σπύρου; Who is Mr. Spirou?
pyos ine o kirios Spiroo?

Masculine and feminine noun endings

On Monday you met some neuter nouns and their typical endings.

Feminine nouns have the following endings: **η,α**, e.g.:

η αδελφή	*i aτΗelfi*	the sister
η θάλασσα	*i thalassa*	the sea

Masculine nouns have three typical endings: **ος, ας, ης**, e.g.:

ο δρόμος	*o τΗromos*	the road
ο άνδρας	*o andras*	the man/husband
ο χάρτης	*o hartis*	the map

Table of noun endings

Here is a table of the endings you have encountered so far:

	nominative	accusative	genitive
Masculine sing.	**-ος/-ας/-ης** *-os/-as/-is*	**-ο/-α/-η** *-o/-a/-i*	**-ου/-α/-η** *-oo/-a/-i*
Masculine pl.	**-οι/-ες/-ες** *-i/-es/-es*	**-ους/-ες/-ες** *-oos/-es/-es*	**-ων/-ών/-ών** *-on/-on/-on*
Feminine sing.	**-α/-η** *-a/-i*	**-α/-η** *-a/-i*	**-ας/-ης** *-as/-is*
Feminine pl.	**-ες/-ες** *-es/-es*	**-ες/-ες** *-es/-es*	**-ων/-ων** *-on/-on*
Neuter sing.	**-ο/-ι/-μα** *-o/-i/-ma*	**-ο/-ι/-μα** *-o/-i/-ma*	**-ου/-ου/-ματος** *-oo/-oo/-matos*
Neuter pl.	**-α/-α/-ματα** *-a/-a/-mata*	**-α/-α/-ματα** *-a/-a/-mata*	**-ων/-ων/-ματων** *-on/-on/-maton*

things to do

2.2 Complete the sentences in Greek and answer the questions, using the schedule:

1 (What time/arrives) το πρώτο
λεωφορείο;

2 Τι ώρα (leaves) το δεύτερο
λεωφορείο;

3 (How long/takes) το λεωφορείο;

4 (How many buses go) στη
Ραφήνα;

δρομολόγιο schedule το λεωφορείο για τη Ραφήνα bus to Rafina	
ΑΝΑΧΩΡΗΣΕΙΣ	ΑΦΙΞΕΙΣ
departure	arrival
9:15	10:30
10:45	12:15
12:15	13:45
14:30	16:00
16:15	17:45

2.3 Tell the times on the clocks shown, then choose a time of day from the list below that goes with each clock.

a.m.

1 ⏰ 03.00

2 ① 08.30

3 `11 55` 11.55

p.m.

4 ① 12.00

5 `14 30` 14.30

6 `18 30` 18.30

το πρωί   to proi
το απόγευμα   to apoyevma

το μεσημέρι   to mesimeri
το βράδυ   to vraτΗi

EATING AND DRINKING

Going out for a drink Greek cafés are open all day and evening, serving coffee, soft drinks, alcoholic drinks, pastries, and ice cream.

Greek coffee As you'll see in the first dialogue, Greek coffee ελληνικός καφές/ *ellinikos kafes* comes in three types:

σκέτος	*sketos*	no sugar
μέτριος	*metrios*	medium sweet
γλυκός	*glikos*	sweet

Note in the dialogue that when you order, the coffee is in the accusative case, so the final -*s* is left off. For more than one coffee the accusative plural ending becomes -ους -*oos*, e.g., δύο μέτριους ΤΗίο *metrioos*. See p. 25 for more information.
The coffee grounds remain in the bottom half of the cup, so be careful not to swallow them! Coffee usually is accompanied by a welcoming glass of cold water – it's safe to drink. Bottled water is available everywhere.
You can also have instant coffee – called νες *nes* (short for νεσκαφέ *Nescafe*), either hot or cold. The latter is called φραπέ *frappé*, and is served with ice and a straw.
Amstel is the local brand of beer, in half-liter bottles – foreign beers are increasingly available. Don't forget that μπύρα *bira* is feminine, so you say μία μπύρα *mia bira*. Plural μπύρες *bires*.
Greek wines Try ρετσίνα retsina, the distinctive resinated wine of Greece (usually white) – it may taste strange at first, but it goes with everything! Available in bottles or copper quarter, half, and liter flasks. Try it with soda to make a longer drink.
Most people know Δεμέστιχα ΤΗemestica – red and white and rosé – always a good, refreshing taste.

Cheers! To say "cheers," simply raise your glass, clink it with everyone else's around the table and say Στην υγειά μας *stin iyia mas* or γεια μας *ya mas*. This literally means "to our health."

Στην υγειά σου *stin iyia soo* or γειά σου *ya soo,* means "to your health."

Asking for the bill When you've finished your drink or meal, attract the waiter's attention by calling κύριε/ *kirie,* or saying παρακαλώ/ *parakalo.*

To ask for the bill, say **Το λογαριασμό, παρακαλώ/** to logariasmo, parakalo.

If you are a bit hesitant to speak, or the waiter is some distance away, do what most people do and, when you've caught his eye, make as if you are writing in the air. You'll soon be doing this like a native!

Tipping Service is always included in the bill, so there is no need to add 15 percent automatically. Just round up what you give to the nearest 50 or 100 drachmas. If you have some coins in change, leave them for the boy who clears away the table.

Φέρτε μας μια μπύρα/Bring us a beer

Peter got up late and is now settling down to one of life's great pleasures in Greece – sitting at a café and watching the world go by. It's hot, but Peter wants to have a Greek coffee.

Waiter: Καλημέρα κύριε. **Τι θα πάρετε;**
        kalimera kirie. ti tha parete?
Peter: Ένα καφέ **παρακαλώ.**
        ena kafe, parakalo.
Waiter: Τι καφέ θέλετε **ελληνικό ή νες;**
        ti kafe thelete elliniko i nes?
Peter: **Δώστε μου** ένα ελληνικό.
        THOste moo ena elliniko.

Waiter:	Σκέτο, μέτριο, ή γλυκό;
	sketo, metrio i gliko?
Peter:	Μέτριο παρακαλώ.
	metrio parakalo.
Waiter:	Αμέσως.
	amesos.

At the next table . . .

Kostas:	Κάνει πολύ ζέστη σήμερα. Διψάω πολύ.
	kani poli zesti simera. ᴛʜ*ipsao poli.*
Maria:	**Κύριε, φέρτε μας μια**
	kirie, ferte mas mia
	μπύρα και μία πορτοκαλάδα.
	*bira ke mia portokala*ᴛʜ*a.*
Waiter:	Μάλιστα.
	malista.
Peter:	**Συγνώμη, έχετε φωτιά . . . ;**
	signomi, ehete fotya . . . ?

Words and phrases from the dialogue

Τι θα πάρετε;	*ti tha parete?*	What will you have (take)?
δώστε μου	ᴛʜ*oste moo*	give me
φέρτε μου	*ferte moo*	bring me
αμέσως	*amesos*	at once/right away
κάνει πολύ ζέστη	*kani poli zesti*	it's very hot (weather)
σήμερα	*simera*	today
διψάω	*thipsao*	I'm thirsty
μία μπύρα	*mia bira*	a beer
παγωμένος,η,ο	*pagomenos -i -o*	cold/chilled
μία πορτοκαλάδα	*mia portokala*ᴛʜ*a*	an orangeade (carbonated)
μάλιστα	*malista*	of course
Έχετε φωτιά;	*ehete fotya?*	Do you have a light?

Drinks and snacks

ο καπουτσίνο	*o kapootsino*	capuccino
ο εσπρέσσο	*o espresso*	espresso
η λεμονάδα	*i lemona*ᴛʜ*a*	lemonade
η σόδα	*i so*ᴛʜ*a*	soda water
το ούζο	*to oozo*	ouzo
το κονιάκ	*to koniak*	brandy
το κρασί	*to krasi*	wine
κόκκινο	*kokkino*	red
άσπρο	*aspro*	white
ροζέ	*roze*	rosé
το παγωτό	*to pagoto*	ice cream
η πάστα	*i pasta*	cake
ο μπακλαβάς	*o baklavas*	baklava
το σάντουίτς	*to sandooits*	sandwich

| Που είναι οι τουαλέττες; | *poo ine i tooalettes?* | Where are the toilets? |

Talking about the weather

Τι καιρό κάνει;	ti kero kani?	What's the weather like?
Ο καιρός είναι καλός/ άσχημος.	o keros ine kalos/ askimos.	The weather is good/ bad.
Κάνει κρύο/ζέστη.	kani krio/zesti.	It's cold/hot.
Έχει ήλιο.	ehi ilio.	It's sunny.
Έχει συννεφιά.	ehi sinefia.	It's cloudy.
Βρέχει.	vrehi.	It's raining.
Φυσάει.	fisai.	It's windy.
ο καύσονας	o kafsonas	heatwave
το δελτίο καιρού	to THeltio keroo	weather forecast
η θάλασσα είναι ήσυχη ταραγμένη.	i THalassa ine isihi/ taragmeni.	The sea is calm/ rough.
Έχει δροσιά.	ehi THrosia.	It's cool.

the way it works

Orders and instructions

In the first dialogue Peter tells the waiter to give him a Greek coffee (by the way, in Greece you can be quite direct with orders, and don't need the "politeness" of, e.g., the English "could I please have . . . ") The grammatical term for an order is the imperative.

This is how some common Greek verbs form their imperative:

First person present		*Polite/Plural imperative*		
φέρνω	ferno	φέρτε	ferte	bring
πηγαίνω	piyeno	πηγαίνετε	piyenete	go
δίνω	THino	δώστε	THoste	give
έρχομαι	erhome	ελάτε	elate	come
κάθομαι	kaTHome	καθίστε	kathiste	sit
παίρνω	perno	πάρτε	parte	take
περιμένω	perimeno	περιμένετε	perimenete	wait
αφήνω	afino	αφίστε	afiste	leave
λέω	leo	πέστε	peste	say
στρίβω	strivo	στρίψτε	stripste	turn
περνάω	pernao	περάστε	peraste	pass
δοκιμάζω	THOkimazo	δοκιμάστε	THOkimaste	try

Verbs ending in *-άω/-ao*

Unlike **θέλω** *thelo*, **κάνω** *kano*, **ξέρω** *ksero*, **καταλαβαίνω** *katalaveno*, there is a group of verbs which end in *-αω* -ao in the first person singular present tense. In this unit you've seen **διψάω** *THipsao*, I'm thirsty, and will encounter **πεινάω** *pinao*, I'm hungry, later.

Another useful verb is **μιλάω** *milao*, I speak.

Here are the present tense endings:

-αω	-ao	μιλάω	milao	I speak
-ας	-as	μιλάς	milas	you speak
-αει	-ai	μιλάει	milai	he/she speaks
-αμε	-ame	μιλάμε	milame	we speak
-ατε	-ate	μιλάτε	milate	you speak
-αν(ε)	-ane	μιλάν(ε)	milan(e)	they speak

Μιλάτε Ελληνικά; Ναί, μιλάω λίγο
milate ellinika? ne, milao ligo

Do you speak Greek?
Yes, I speak a little

Διψάς Μαρία; Ναι, θέλω ένα ποτήρι νερό παρακαλώ.
thipsas Maria? ne, thelo ena potiri nero parakalo

Are you thirsty, Maria?
Yes, I want a glass of
water, please

Eating out

Greece is full of every variety of eating place, from the street
seller of grilled ears of corn, or bread sticks *(koulouria),* to the
smartest hotel restaurant. Although fast food places are springing
up everywhere, the traditional eating place is the taverna –
usually a simple, no-fuss family restaurant with a limited menu of
dishes.

The normal thing to do when you go to a taverna is to go into
the kitchen and select what you want to eat – if you're having
fish you can have it weighed and a price quoted.

Incidentally, the best fast food in Greece is the *souvlaki*
σουβλάκι, a few skewers of pork pieces in pita bread with salad,
bought from a small snack bar on the street. They are delicious
and filling.

Most Greeks have a late lunch around 1:30–2:00 pm, a siesta for
a few hours, then back to work, before a late-night supper
around 9 pm or 10 pm.

On the road, you'll see grill houses called **ψησταριά** *psistaria,*
where a limited range of grilled meat dishes is available.

Larger restaurants are called **Εστιατόριο** *estiatorio,* where a
wider range of dishes is available.

Πάμε μαζί/Let's go together

Peter wants to find somewhere to eat, and asks his new friends for a recommendation.

Peter: Κώστα, **υπάρχει μια καλή ταβέρνα εδώ κοντά;**
Kosta, iparhi mia kali taverna ετΗο *konda?*

Costas: Ναι, βέβαια. Υπάρχει μια πολύ καλή. Την λένε τα "Τρία αδέλφια".
ne, vevea. iparhi mia poli kali. tin lene ta tria αΤΗelfia.
Τρώμε εκεί κάθε βράδυ.
trome eki kathe vraΤΗi.

Maria: Πάμε μαζί απόψε;
pame mazi apopse?

Costas: Μαρία δεν ξέρω...
Maria, then ksero . . .

Peter: **Θαυμάσια ιδέα.** Τι ώρα λοιπόν;
thavmasia ithea. ti ora lipon?

Words and phrases from the dialogue

Υπάρχει . . . ;	*iparhi . . . ?*	is there . . . ?
Υπάρχουν . . . ;	*iparhoon . . . ?*	are there . . . ?
Εδώ κοντά	ετΗο *konda*	near here
Βέβαια	*vevea*	certainly
Τα τρία αδέλφια	*Ta tria* αΤΗelfia	"The Three Brothers"
τρώμε εκεί	*trome eki*	we eat there
σχεδόν	*sk*eΤΗon	nearly
κάθε βράδυ	*kathe* vraΤΗi	every evening
πάμε μαζί	*pame mazi*	let's go together
απόψε	*apopse*	tonight
δεν ξέρω	ΤΗen *ksero*	I don't know
θαυμάσια ιδέα	ΤΗavmasia iΤΗea	great idea
τι ώρα;	*ti ora?*	what time?
λοιπόν	*lipon*	well/anyway/now then

Ένα τραπέζι για τρεις;/A table for three?

Peter, Maria, and Costas meet at the Three Brothers taverna.

Waiter: Καλησπέρα σας. Ένα τραπέζι για τρείς;
kalispera sas. ena trapezi ya tris?

Maria: Ναι, ένα καλό τραπ έξι για τον Άγγλο μας.
ne, ena kalo trapezi ya ton anglo mas.

Kostas: Μας δίνετε τον κατάλογο, σας παρακαλώ.
mas ΤΗ*inete ton katalogo, sas parakalo.*

Maria: Φέρτε μας μερικούς μεζέδες πρώτα. Ένα τζατζίκι, μία
*ferte mas merikous meze*ΤΗes *prota. ena tzatziki, mia*
ταραμοσαλάτα και μία χωριάτικη.
taramosalata ke mia horiatiki.

Costas: Τι ψάρια έχετε;
      ti psaria ehete?
Waiter: Έχουμε ξιφία μπαρμπούνια και καλαμαράκια.
      ehoome ksifia, barboonya ke kalamarakya.
Maria: Peter, προτιμάς ψάρι ή κρέας;
      Peter, protimas psari i kreas?
Peter: Κρέας νομίζω. Πεινάω σαν λύκος. Μ'αρέσει πολύ το σουβλάκι.
      kreas nomizo. pinao san likos. m'aresi poli to soovlaki.
Waiter: Είστε έτοιμοι;
      iste etimi?
Maria: Ναι. Λοιπόν θα πάρουμε ένα σουβλάκι, μία καλαμαράκια, και
      ne. lipon tha paroome ena soovlaki, mia kalamarakya, ke
      ένα ξιφία και δύο πατάτες τηγανητές.
      ena ksifia ke THio patates tiganites.
Waiter: Τι θα πιείτε;
      ti tha pyite?
Costas: Φέρτε μας ένα μπουκάλι Ρετσίνα. Ελληνικό φαΐ χωρίς κρασί!;
      ferte mas ena bookali retsina. (turning to the others) elliniko
      fai horis krasi?!

Cheval!

AXAPNΩN 282
ΠΙΤΣΑΡΙΑ-ΕΣΤΙΑΤΟΡΙΟ
THΛ. 864 2258

ΤΟ CHEVAL ΚΑΘΕ ΜΕΡΑ, ΜΕΣΗΜΕΡΙ ΚΑΙ ΒΡΑΔΥ
ΣΑΣ ΠΡΟΣΦΕΡΕΙ ΜΙΑ ΜΕΓΑΛΗ ΠΟΙΚΙΛΙΑ ΦΑΓΗΤΩΝ,
ΣΕ ΦΘΗΝΕΣ ΤΙΜΕΣ ΚΑΙ ΓΡΗΓΟΡΗ ΕΞΥΠΗΡΕΤΗΣΗ.

ΤΙΜΟΚΑΤΑΛΟΓΟΣ ΓΙΑ ΤΟ ΣΠΙΤΙ

ΠΙΤΣΕΣ

● ΤΥΡΙ, σάλτσα	530
● ΖΑΜΠΟΝ, τυρί, σάλτσα	550
(καί όλες οι πίτσες μ' ένα είδος)	550
● ΖΑΜΠΟΝ, μπέικον, τυρί, σάλτσα	580
(καί όλες οι πίτσες μ' ένα είδος)	580
● ΤΟΝΟΣ, κλπ.	600
● SPECIAL (απ' όλα)	600
● SUPER SPECIAL	620

ΖΥΜΑΡΙΚΑ

● ΝΑΠΟΛΙ σάλτσα, τυρί, σπαγγέτι, λαζάνια	210
● ΜΠΟΛΩΝΕΖ σάλτσα, τυρί, σπαγγέτι, λαζάνια	300
● SPECIAL μακαρόνια, ζαμπόν, μπέικον, μανιτάρια	320
● ΡΙΓΓΑΤΟΝΙ 4 τυριά	370
● ΚΑΝΕΛΛΟΝΙΑ	400
● ΒΟΥΤΥΡΟΥ σπαγγέτι, λαζάνια	180

ΣΑΛΑΤΕΣ

● ΡΑΨΩΔΙΑ μικρή	320
● ΡΑΨΩΔΙΑ μεγάλη	400
● ΧΩΡΙΑΤΙΚΗ	220
● ΛΑΧΑΝΟΚΗΠΟΣ	220
● ΡΟΖ ΣΑΛΑΤΑ	260
● ΠΡΑΣΙΝΗ ΣΑΛΑΤΑ	140
● ΚΟΚΚΙΝΗ, άστρη, εποχής	240
● ΡΩΣΣΙΚΗ	150
● ΠΑΤΑΤΟΣΑΛΑΤΑ	150
● ΜΕΛΙΤΖΑΝΟΣΑΛΑΤΑ	150
● ΤΖΑΤΖΙΚΙ	150

ΔΙΑΦΟΡΑ

● ΜΑΝΙΤΑΡΙΑ τηγανιτά	300
● ΠΑΤΑΤΕΣ	90
● ΤΥΡΙ φέτα	130
● ΡΟΚΦΟΡ	170
● ΚΕΦΑΛΟΓΡΑΒΙΕΡΑ	160

ΤΗΣ ΩΡΑΣ

● ΜΠΙΦΤΕΚΙ σχάρας	360
● ΜΠΙΦΤΕΚΙ chef, Cheval	440
● ΜΠΙΦΤΕΚΙ με αυγά	460
● ΣΥΚΩΤΙ σχάρας	450
● ΦΙΛΕΤΟ σχάρας	640
● ΧΟΙΡΙΝΗ - ΜΟΣΧΑΡΙΣΙΑ σχάρας	460
● ΣΟΥΒΛΑΚΙ	520
● ΣΑΓΑΝΑΚΙ	320
● ΟΜΕΛΕΤΕΣ διάφορες	280
● ΟΜΕΛΕΤΕΣ complé	320
● ΣΑΝΤΟΥΙΤΣ	160
● ΠΑΣΤΕΣ	125

Restaurant menu items

τζατζίκι	*tzatziki*	yoghurt, cucumber, garlic dip
χωριάτικη	*horiatiki*	country salad, with feta cheese
καλαμαράκια	*kalamarakia*	little squids, fried whole
ξιφίας	*ksifias*	swordfish
μπαρμπούνια	*barboonya*	red mullet – usually priced by the kilo, which is enough for 3 or 4 people

Words and phrases from the dialogue

ένα τραπέζι για τρείς	ena trapezi ya tris	a table for three
για τον Άγγλο μας	ya ton anglo mas	for our Englishman
μας δίνετε	mas THinete	give us
ο κατάλογος	o katalogos	the menu
μερικοί, ές, ά	meriki/es/a	some
μεζέδες	mezeTHes	appetizers
πρώτα	prota	first
Τι ψάρια έχετε;	ti psaria ehete?	What fish do you have?
Προτιμάς...ή...	protimas . . . i . . . ?	Do you prefer . . . or . . . ?
κρέας	kreas	meat
νομίζω	nomizo	I think
πεινάω (σαν λύκος)	pinao (san likos)	I'm hungry (as a wolf)
μ'αρέσει	m'aresi	I like (sing.)
μ'αρέσουν	m'aresoon	I like (plural)
το σουβλάκι	to soovlaki	kebab
Είστε έτοιμοι;	iste etimi?	Are you ready?
θα πάρουμε	tha paroome	We'll take/have . . .
πατάτες τηγανητές	patates tiganites	french fries
τι θα πιείτε;	ti tha pyite?	What will you drink?
ένα μπουκάλι ρετσίνα	ena bookali retsina	a bottle of retsina
το ελληνικό φαί	to elliniko fai	Greek food
χωρίς	horis	without
το κρασί	to krasi	wine

Other useful phrases

Μπορώ να κλείσω ένα τραπέζι;	boro na kliso ena trapezi?	Can I reserve a table?
Μπορώ να δω τι έχετε;	boro na THo ti ehete?	Can I see what you have?
Ελάτε στην κουζίνα.	elate stin koozina.	Come into the kitchen.
πιάτο της ημέρας	piato tis imeras	dish of the day
κουβέρ	koover	cover charge
Μπορώ να παραγγείλω;	boro na parangilo?	Can I order?
Λίγο νερό παρακαλώ	ligo nero, parakalo.	Some water, please.
ορεκτικά	orektika	appetizers
κύριο πιάτο	kirio piato	main course
έπιδόρπιο	epiTHorpio	dessert
το λογαριασμό, παρακαλώ.	to logariasmo, parakalo.	The bill, please.
Μου εξηγείτε το λογαριασμό;	moo eksiyite to logariasmo?	Can you explain the bill?
Μήπως κάνατε λάθος.	mipos kanate lathos.	Maybe you've made a mistake.

See topic vocabulary, pages 98–100, for names of food, drink, vegetables, etc.

the way it works

Personal pronouns

On Monday you saw the nominative (subject form of the noun) forms of the personal pronouns, e.g.: Εγώ *ego*, εσύ/ *esi*. In the first dialogue, μου *moo* and μας *mas* (me and us) – in δώστε μου *THoste moo* and φέρτε μας *ferte mas* – are in the genitive case. This case is used after verbs like give, bring, tell, etc. (where we often use "to" in English) as well as signifying possession (see the Introduction and Tuesday, page 26).

Here is a complete table of all the personal pronouns in the three cases:

nominative		accusative		genitive	
εγώ	ego	με/(ε)μένα	me/(e)mena	μου	moo
εσύ	esi	σε/(ε)σένα	se/(e)sena	σου	soo
αυτός	aftos	τον/αυτόν	ton/afton	του	too
αυτή	afti	το/αυτό	tin/aftin	της	tis
αυτό	afto	το/αυτό	to/afto	του	too
εμείς	emis	μας/(ε)μας	mas/(e)mas	μας	mas
εσείς	esis	σας/(ε)σας	sas/(e)sas	σας	sas
αυτοί	afti	τους/αυτούς	toos/aftoos	τους	toos
αυτές	aftes	τις/αυτές	tis/aftes	τους	toos
αυτά	afta	τα/αυτά	ta/afta	τους	toos

Examples:

Δώστε του τον καφέ.
THoste too ton kafe.

Give him the coffee.

Συγνώμη, φέρτε μου κι ένα παγωτό.
Signomi, ferte moo ke ena pagoto.

Sorry, bring me an ice cream as well.

Την περιμένω στη στάση κάθε πρωί.
tin perimeno sti stasi kaTHe proi.

I wait for her at the bus stop every morning.

Τους βλέπω κάθε μέρα.
toos vlepo kathe mera.

I see them every day.

Note the position of the personal pronoun before the verb.

After a preposition, e.g., για *ya* (for), the longer form of the accusative personal pronoun is used.

Η μπύρα είναι για μένα, η πορτοκαλάδα είναι για αυτήν. The beer is for me, the *i bira ine ya mena, i portokalatha* orangeade is for her. *ine ya aftin.*

things to do

3.1   Order the following kinds of coffee and cold drinks:

1   medium

2   plain sweet

3   2 medium

4   a beer

5   2 beers

6   3 cokes

3.2   Try to complete this dialogue in a cafe:

You: (The bill, please)
Waiter: **Μάλιστα, δύο μπύρες και δύο τοστ.**
         malista, THio bires ke THio tost.
You: (say you're sorry, but the order is 2 beers, 1 toast)
Waiter: **Λυπάμαι έχετε δίκιο.**
         lipame, ehete THikio.
You: (ask how much)
Waiter: **Τριακόσιες ογδόντα δραχμές.**
         triakosies ogTHonda THrahmes.
You: (offer 400 dr and say he can keep the change).

3.3   Try to complete this dialogue in a restaurant:

ΚΑΤΑΛΟΓΟΣ MENU	
ΟΡΕΚΤΙΚΑ	
Καλαμαράκια	500 δρχ
Χταπόδι	250
Ταραμοσαλάτα	150
Τζατζίκι	150
Χωριάτικη	300
Πατάτες τιγανητές	200
ΨΑΡΙΑ	
Ξιφίας	750
Μπαρμπούνια	5.000
ΚΡΑΣΙΑ	
Δεμέστιχα	500 δρχ
Ρετσίνα	200
Μπύρα	120
Κοκα-κόλα	100
Σόδα	80

Waiter: **Είστε έτοιμοι;**
         iste etimi?
You: (1 squid, 1 octopus 1 tara)
Waiter: **Και μετά;**
         ke meta?
You: (half kilo of red mullet, and two orders of french fries)
Waiter: **Εντάξει, τι θα πιείτε;**
         endaksi, ti tha pyite?
You: (bottle of retsina and 1 soda)
Waiter: **Αμέσως.**
         amesos.
You: (and a Greek salad, please)
Waiter: **Εντάξει.**
         endaksi.

If your math is good, add up your order and say how much your bill is in Greek money!

BANK AND POST OFFICE

Banks and exchanges Look for the word **ΤΡΑΠΕΖΑ** *trapeza*, which means bank, and **ΣΥΝΑΛΛΑΓΜΑ** *synallagma*, which means exchange.

Banking hours in the city are usually 8:30 am to 2:00 pm.

Some banks in Greece have extended hours for exchanging foreign currency. You also can obtain money 24 hours a day by using automated currency machines or by using ATMs.

To change traveler's checks you'll need your passport. In most banks a clerk will carry out the transaction, then you go to a separate cashier (**TAMEIO** *tamio*) to get your money.

On the islands there are often many exchange offices available, as well as banks, that are open mornings and evenings.

θέλω να χαλάσω εκατό λίρες
I want to change £100

Anne wants to change some traveler's checks and send postcards home. She first goes to the bank.

Clerk: Παρακαλώ.
parakalo.

Anne: **Θέλω να χαλάσω μερικά traveler's checks**
thelo na halaso merika travelers checks.

Clerk: Πόσα τσεκ έχετε;
Posa tsek ehete?

Anne: **Δύο τσεκ εκατό λίρες το καθένα. Διακόσιες λίρες.**
THio tsek ekato lires to kathena. THiakosies lires.

Clerk: **Το διαβατήριό σας παρακαλώ. Ποιά είναι η διεύθυνσή σας;**
to THiavatirio sas parakalo. pya ine i THiefthinsi sas?

Anne: Μένω στο ξενοδοχείο Ακρόπολη οδός Μητσαίων δέκα εφτά.
meno sto ksenoTHohio akropoli oTHos mitseon THeka efta.

Clerk: Υπογράψτε εδώ,και μετά πηγαίνετε στο ταμείο απέναντι.
ipograpste eTHo, ke meta piyenete sto tamio apenandi.

Anne: Εντάξει ευχαριστώ. Συγνώμη, που είναι το ταχυδρομείο;
endaksi efharisto. signomi, poo ine to tahiTHromio?

Words and phrases from the dialogue

μερικά	*merika*	some
θέλω να χαλάσω	*thelo na halaso*	I want to change
Πόσα τσεκ έχετε;	*possa tsek ehete?*	How many checks have you got?
εκατό λίρες το καθένα	*ekato lires to kathena*	£100 each
το διαβατήριό σας	*to THiavatirio sas*	your passport
η διεύθυνσή σας	*i thiefthinsi sas*	your address
υπογράψτε εδώ	*ipograpste eTHo*	sign here
πηγαίνετε	*piyenete*	go
το ταμείο	*to tamio*	cashier
απέναντι	*apenandi*	opposite
Μένω...οδός	*Meno . . . oTHos*	I'm living/staying . . .
Μητσαίων 17	*Mitseon 17*	17 Mitseon Street
το ταχυδρομείο	*to tahiTHromio*	post office

Other useful words and phrases

πιστωτική κάρτα	*pistotiki karta*	credit card
το νόμισμα	*to nomisma*	coin
το χαρτονόμισμα	*to hartonomisma*	bill
το τσεκ/η επιταγή	*to tsek/i epitayi*	check
το βιβλίο επιταγών	*to vivlio epitagon*	checkbook
Πόσο έχει το δολλάριο σήμερα;	*poso ehi to THolario simera?*	What's the rate of the dollar today?
Συμπληρώστε αυτό το έντυπο. *simbliroste afto to endipo.*		Fill out this form.
Που να υπογράψω; *poo na ipograpso?*		Where do I sign?

Μου δίνετε γραμματόσημα;
Give me some stamps

Anne goes to the post office.

Anne: Θέλω να στείλω έξι κάρτες στην Αγγλία. **Μου δίνετε**
thelo na stilo eksi kartes stin anglia. moo THinete
γραμματόσημα παρακαλώ;
grammatosima parakalo?

Clerk: Μάλιστα. Έξι γραμματόσημα εξήντα δραχμές το ένα.
malista. eksi grammatosima eksinda THrahmes to ena.
Τριακόσιες εξήντα δραχμές όλα μαζί.
triakosies eksinda THrahmes ola mazi.

Anne: Εντάξει. Ορίστε.
endaksi. oriste.

Clerk: Ορίστε τα ρέστα σας.
oriste ta resta sas.

Anne: **Συγνώμη, θέλω να τηλεφωνήσω στην Αγγλία.**
Signomi, thelo na tilefoniso stin anglia.

ΤΑΧΥΔΡΟΜΙΚΟΝ
ΤΑΜΙΕΥΤΗΡΙΟΝ

Words and phrases from the dialogue

θέλω να στείλω	*thelo na stilo*	I want to send
έξη κάρτες	*eksi kartes*	6 postcards
το/τα γραμματόσημο -α	*to/ta grammatosimo -a*	stamp(-s)
όλα μαζί	*ola mazi*	all together
τα ρέστα σας	*ta resta sas*	your change
θέλω να τηλεφωνήσω	*thelo na tilefoniso*	I want to make a telephone call

Other useful phrases

το γράμμα/τα γράμματα	*to gramma/ta grammata*	letter/s
ο φάκελλος	*o fakellos*	envelope
το δέμα/τα δέματα	*to THEma/ta THEmata*	parcel/s
το στυλό	*to stilo*	ballpoint pen
το γραμματοκιβώτιο	*to grammatokivotio*	mailbox
αεροπορικός	*aeroporikos*	by air mail
συστημένο	*sistimeno*	registered

Τι ώρα ανοίγει/κλείνει;	*ti ora aniyi/klini?*	What time does it open?/close?
Για που είναι;	*ya poo ine?*	Where is it/are they for (going to)?
Σε ποιό γκισέ;	*se pyo gise?*	At which counter?

For notes on telephoning, see page 79.

the way it works

I want to . . .

Θέλω να THelo na . . .   I want to . . .

After θέλω να thelo na . . . , you will find a different form of the verb used. Notice how in the dialogue Anne says θέλω να χαλάσω *thelo na halaso* – for "I want to change . . . ." In the present tense form the verb would normally be χαλάω *halao*.

See also page 66 for the future with θα *tha*, which uses the same form.

things to do

3.4   At the bank

Put the sentences of this dialogue in the right order.

a   Μάλιστα. Η λίρα έχει 270 δραχμές σήμερα.
b   Που είναι το συνάλλαγμα;
c   Ορίστε-μένω στο ξενοδοχείο "Όμηρος"
d   Το διαβατήριο και τη διεύθυνσή σας παρακαλώ.
e   Απέναντι κύριε, δεξιά.
f   Θέλω να χαλάσω εκατό λίρες.

SHOPPING

Shop opening hours vary from day to day in the summer months:

Monday	8:30 am–3:00 pm	Thursday	8:30 am–1:30 pm,
Tuesday	8:30 am–1:30 pm,		5:30 pm–8:30 pm
	5:30 pm–8:30 pm	Friday	8:30 am–1:30 pm
Wednesday	8:30 am–3:00 pm	Saturday	8:30 am–3:00 pm

In the winter months, shops are generally open from 9:00 am to 7:00 pm.

In resort locations and the islands, shops will have more flexible hours, with souvenir shops, supermarkets, jewelers, and pharmacies open until 10:00 pm or later.

Credit cards are accepted in some tourist shops and in many better hotels and restaurants. But many smaller shops still don't take credit cards. Be sure to have cash on hand for some purchases.

Plaka – "flea market" The most famous shopping area for souvenirs, leather, jewelery, and reproductions of ancient art is the Plaka – at the foot of the Acropolis – easily reached from Syntagma Square. One area, next to the Monastiraki metro station, is called the Flea Market, where antique dealers and bargain-hunters abound.

The main shopping areas of Athens are in Ermou Street (off Syntagma Square), especially for leather, shoes, furs; Stadiou and Panepistimiou. For boutiques and high fashion, Kolonaki Square is for you.

BUYING FOOD

Δώστε μου ένα κιλό/Give me a kilo

Anne is taking the bus to Sounion today and wants to buy food for a picnic on the beach. Her first stop is the bakery (**ο φούρνος** *o foornos*).

Baker: Καλημέρα σας κυρία. Παρακαλώ;
kalimera sas kiria. parakalo?

Anne: **Μία φραντζόλα μαύρο ψωμί παρακαλώ.** Μήπως έχετε τυρόπιτες;
mia frantzola mavro psomi parakalo. mipos ehete tiropittes?

Baker: Βεβαίως. Εδώ είναι κυρία. Είναι πολύ φρέσκες.
veveos. ετηο ine kiria. ine poli freskes.

Anne: Δώστε μου δύο. **Πόσο κάνουν;**
τηoste moo τηio. posso kanoon?

Baker: Εκατόν σαράντα δραχμές.
ekatov saranda τηrahmes.

Anne then goes to the produce market.

Assistant: Ορίστε. Τι φρούτα
oriste. ti froota
θέλετε;
thelete?

Anne: Μ' αρέσουν πολύ τα
m' aresoon poli ta
ροδάκινα. Δώστε μου
roτηakina. τηoste
ένα κιλό.
moo ena kilo.

Assistant: Θέλετε από αυτά ή
thelete apo afta i
από εκείνα;
apo ekina?

Anne: Προτιμώ τα μικρά. Θα
protimo ta mikra. tha
ήθελα και μισό κιλό
ithela ke miso kilo
σταφύλια.
stafilia.

Assistant: Τα μαύρα είναι πιο γλυκά. Δοκιμάστε τα.
ta mavra ine pyo glika. τηokimaste ta.

Anne: Ναι έχετε δίκιο. **Θα πάρω λοιπόν μισό κιλό μαύρα.**
ne, ehete τηikio. tha paro lipon miso kilo mavra.
Πόσο είναι;
poso ine?

Assistant:	Πεντακόσιες σαράντα. Δεν έχετε ψιλά;
	pendakosies saranda. THen ehete psila?
Anne:	Για να δω. Δυστυχώς δεν έχω.
	ya na THO. THistihos THen eho.
Assistant:	Καλά δεν πειράζει. Ορίστε τα ρέστα σας.
	kala THen birazi. oriste ta resta sas.

Words and phrases from the dialogue

ροδάκινα	*roTHakina*	peaches
μια φραντζόλα	*mia frantzla*	a loaf
μαύρο ψωμί	*mavro psomi*	brown bread
Μήπως έχετε;	*mipos ehete?*	Do you have . . . ?
μία τυρόπιτα -ες	*mia tiropitta -es*	cheese pie/s
φρέσκες	*freskes*	fresh (fem./plur.)
Δώστε μου . . .	*THoste moo . . .*	Give me . . .
από αυτά ή από εκείνα	*apo afta i apo ekina*	from these or those
θα ήθελα . . .	*tha ithela . . .*	I'd like . . .
μισό κιλό σταφύλια	*miso kilo stafilia*	half a kilo of grapes
πιο . . . από . . .	*pyo . . . apo . . .*	more . . . than . . .
Δοκιμάστε τα	*THOkimaste ta.*	Try them.
Έχετε δίκιο	*ehete THikio.*	You're right.
Δεν έχετε ψιλά;	*THen ehete psila?*	Don't you have change?
Για να δω	*ya na THO.*	I'll see.
δυστυχώς	*THistihos*	unfortunately
Δεν πειράζει	*THen pirazi*	It doesn't matter.
Προτιμώ τα μικρά.	*protimo ta mikra.*	I prefer the small ones.
τα μαύρα	*ta mavra*	the black ones (grapes)

Other useful words and phrases

Είναι φρέσκο -α;	*ine fresco -a?*	Is it fresh?
Τι είναι αυτό/αυτά;	*ti ine afto/afta?*	What's this/these?
ένα τέταρτο	*ena tetarto*	quarter (kilo)
ένα λίτρο	*ena litro*	liter
ένα πακέτο	*ena paketo*	packet
μία κονσέρβα	*mia conserva*	can
μία φέτα	*mia feta*	slice
ένα κομμάτι	*ena kommati*	piece
αρκετό -ά	*arketo -a*	enough
πάρα πολύ	*para poli*	very much
Τιποτ' άλλο;	*tipot' allo?*	Anything else?
Αυτά.	*afta.*	That's it/that's all.
μία σακούλα	*mia sakoola*	a plastic carrier bag

Notice that after a quantity word like **κιλό** *kilo*, **λίτρο** *litro*, **πακέτο** *paketo*, the item or items are always in the nominative case, singular or plural. See topic vocabulary page 97 for names of food, fruit, vegetable, meat, and food shops.

AT THE PHARMACY

There are many pharmacies in
Greece – recognizable
by the sign:

and the lettering: **ΦΑΡΜΑΚΕΙΟ**

The *Athens News* (a daily, except Monday, paper in English) has
a list of pharmacies on night duty if you need items on the
weekend or during the night.

The pharmacist/owner is always qualified, and is able to give
advice, take blood pressure, and give injections, if necessary. On
islands and in resorts, your two most important purchases will be
effective suntan lotion and protection from mosquitoes. For the
latter, buy a **Σπιρα-μάτ** *Spira-Mat* burner, plus tablets that are
changed daily.

Με πονάει η πλάτη μου/My back hurts

Peter needs a few things from the pharmacy.

Assistant: Ορίστε. Τι θέλετε;
oriste. ti thelete?

Peter: **Με πονάει η πλάτη μου από τον ήλιο.**
me ponai i plati moo apo ton ilio.

Assistant: Αυτή η κρέμα είναι πολύ καλή. Βάλτε την τρεις φορές την ημέρα.
afti i krema ine poli kali. valte tin tris fores tin imera.

Peter: Ευχαριστώ. Πόσο είναι;
efharisto. posso ine?

Assistant: Μόνο τριακόσιες πενήντα δραχμές. **Τιποτ' άλλο;**
mono triakoses peninda тнrahmes. tipot' allo?

Peter: Τι έχετε για κουνούπια;
ti ehete ya koonoopia?

Assistant: Δοκιμάστε αυτό το σπρέι. Έχουμε και το Σπιρα-Μάτ.
тнokimaste afto to sprei. Ehoome ke to "Spira-Mat."

Peter: Εντάξει. Θα πάρω το σπρέι. **Μου δίνετε κι ένα κουτί
ασπιρίνες και ένα αντιηλιακό λάδι.**
*endaksi. tha paro to sprei. moo thinete ki ena kooti
aspirines ke ena andiliako laтнi.*

Assistant: Μάλιστα. Όλα μαζί κάνουν δύο χιλιάδες τριακόσιες δραχμές.
malista. ola mazi kanoun тнio hiliaтнes triakosies тнrahmes.

Peter: **Πιο αργά, παρακαλώ.** Ο πονοκέφαλος μου κάνει τα
Pyo arga, parakalo. O ponokefalos moo kani ta
Ελληνικά πιο δύσκολα.
ellinika pyo тнiskola.

Phrases from the dialogue

Με πονάει η πλάτη μου	*me ponai i plati moo.*	My back hurts.
από τον ήλιο	*apo ton ilio*	from the sun
βάλτε την	*valte tin*	put it (on)
τρείς φορές την ημέρα	*tris fores tin imera*	3 times a day
για κουνούπια	*ya koonoopia*	for mosquitoes
ένα κουτί ασπιρίνες	*ena kooti aspirines*	box of aspirin
ένα αντιηλιακό λάδι	*ena andiliako laтнi*	suntan oil
ένα σπρέυ	*ena sprei*	a spray
ο πονοκέφαλος	*o ponokefalos*	headache

Other useful words and phrases

διανυκτερεύον φαρμακείο	*тнianikterevon farmakio*	all-night pharmacy
το κρυολόγημα	*to krioloyima*	cold
ο βήχας	*o vihas*	cough
το αλλεργικό συνάχι	*to alleryiko sinahi*	hay fever
το έγκαυμα του ηλίου	*to engavma too ilioo*	sunburn
η ναυτία	*i naftia*	motion sickness
η διάρροια	*i тнiaria*	diarrhea
η συνταγή	*i sindayi*	prescription

Μπορώ να το πάρω χωρίς συνταγή;
boro na to paro horis sindayi?
Μπορείτε να μου ετοιμάσετε αυτή τη συνταγή;
borite na moo etimasete afti ti sindayi?
Πότε θα είναι έτοιμη;
pote tha ine etimi?

Can I take it without a
  prescription?
Can you fill this
  prescription?
When will it be ready?

See Saturday for phrases concerning emergencies, illness, etc., and Topic Vocabulary pages 96 and 100 for toiletries, parts of the body, etc.

the way it works

I like/I don't like

As you saw on pages 50–51, to say you like something, you use the phrase **μ' αρέσει** *m'aresi* in Greek.

Notice that the thing or things you like are in the nominative case, as it is/they are the subject of the sentence. The person doing the liking is in the accusative (literally: "it pleases me").

Singular

μ'αρέσει ο/η/το	*m'aresi o/i/to*	I like
σ'αρέσει	*s'aresi*	you like
του/της αρέσει	*too/tis aresi*	he/she likes
μας αρέσει	*mas aresi*	we like
σας αρέσει	*sas aresi*	you like
τους αρέσει	*toos aresi*	they like

Plural

Μ'αρέσουν(ε) οι/οι/τα	*m'aresoon(e) i/i/ta*	I like
σ΄αρέσουν(ε)	*s'aresoon(e)*	you like
του/της αρέσουν(ε)	*too/tis aresoon(e)*	he/she likes
μας αρέσουν(ε)	*mas aresoon(e)*	we like
σας αρέσουν(ε)	*sas aresoon(e)*	you like
τους αρέσουν(ε)	*toos aresoon(e)*	they like

Some examples:

Μ΄αρέσει πολύ η ελληνική μουσική.
m'aresi poli i elliniki moosiki.
I like Greek music very much.

Σ'αρέσουν οι ντολμάδες;
s'aresoon i dolmaτμes?
Do you like dolmathes (stuffed vine leaves)?

Δεν μας αρέσει το ούζο.
τΗen mas aresi to oozo.
We don't like ouzo. (They don't know what they're missing!)

To make this expression negative – I don't like – simply put the word δεν *τΗen* in front, e. g., **δεν μ΄αρέσει** *τΗen m'aresi.*

Comparatives

When you want to say that something is, for example, cheaper or smaller than something else in Greek there is one easy way to do it.

The word πιο *pyo* before an adjective means "more" – for example:

Αυτά τα παπούτσια είναι πιο φτηνά.
afta ta papootsia ine pyo ftina.
These shoes are cheaper.

Το αυτοκίνητό μου είναι πιο μεγάλο. My car is bigger.
to aftokinito moo ine pyo megalo.

things to do

4.1 **At the pharmacy** Match the articles with the prices in the
price list in Greek opposite:

1	soap 80 dr	**a**	τετρακόσιες εβδομήντα πέντε δραχμές
2	toothpaste 150 dr	**b**	διακόσιες σαράντα δραχμές
3	suntan oil 475 dr	**c**	ογδόντα δραχμές
4	aspirin 240 dr	**d**	εκατόν πενήντα δραχμές

4.2 Practice asking for the quantities of these items:

1 a kilo of apples
2 two cans of tomato juice
3 a box of sugar
4 a liter of water

4.3 Say what you like/don't like:

1 I don't like octopus.
2 I like grapes very much.
3 I like Greek cheese.
4 I don't like Greek cigarettes.

BUYING CLOTHES

Μπορώ να τις δοκιμάσω;/Can I try them on?

Peter needs to get a few extra clothes and heads for the shops.

Peter: **Χρειάζομαι μερικές**
hriazome merikes
μακώ μπλούζες.
mako bloozes.

Assistant: **Τι χρώμα θέλετε;**
ti hroma thelete?

Peter: **Θα ήθελα μία μπλέ**
tha ithela mia ble
και μία κίτρινη.
ke mia kitrini.

Assistant: **Τι μέγεθος είστε;**
ti megethos iste?

Peter: **Στην Αγγλία είμαι μέγεθος σαράντα, αλλά εδώ δεν ξέρω**
stin anglia ime megethos saranda, alla ετηο τηen ksero
τι μέγεθος είμαι. Μπορώ να τις δοκιμάσω;
ti megethos ime. boro na tis τηokimaso?

Assistant: **Βεβαίως. Περάστε στο δοκιμαστήριο.**
veveos. peraste sto τηokimastirio.

Peter: **Η μπλέ είναι πολύ στενή. Έχετε μία πιο μεγάλη;**
i ble ine poli steni. ehete mia pyo megali?

Assistant: **Να κοιτάξω. Η κίτρινη σας έρχεται καλά;**
na kitakso. i kitrini sas erhete kala?

Peter: **Ναι. Νομίζω η κίτρινη είναι εντάξει. Ευχαριστώ! Παίρνετε**
ne. nomizo i kitrini ine endaksi. Efharisto! Pernete
Access;
Access?

Words and phrases from the dialogue

χρειάζομαι	hriazome	I need
μακώ μπλούζα-ες	mako blooza -es	teeshirt/-s
Τι χρώμα;	ti hroma?	What color?
Τι μέγεθος είστε;	ti megethos iste?	What size are you?
Μπορώ να τις δοκιμάσω;	boro na tis τηokimaso?	Can I try them on?
περάστε στο	peraste sto	go through/pass to the
δοκιμαστήριο	τηokimastirio	fitting room
στενός -η -ο	stenos -i -o	tight
πιο μεγάλος -η -ο	pyo megalos -i -o	bigger
να κοιτάξω	na kitakso	I'll have a look
σας έρχεται καλά;	sas erhete kala?	does it suit/fit you?
στο μέγεθός σας	sto megetho sas	in your size
Παίρνετε Visa;	pernete Visa?	Do you take Visa?

Colors

κόκκινος-η -ο	*kokkinos -i -o*	red	άσπρος -η -ο	*aspros -i -o*	white
κίτρινος -η -ο	*kitrinos -i -o*	yellow	μαύρος -η -ο	*mavros -i -o*	black
πράσινος -η -ο	*prasinos -i -o*	green	μπλέ	*ble*	blue

Other useful words and phrases

Απλώς κοιτάω.	*aplos kitao.*	I'm just looking.
τι χρώματα έχετε;	*ti hromata ehete?*	What colors do you have?
σκούρο /ανοιχτό	*scooro/anihto*	dark/light
τι ύφασμα είναι;	*ti ifasma ine?*	What material is it?
μία μπλούζα βαμβακερή	*mia blooza vamvakeri*	cotton blouse
πάρτε μου μέτρα	*parte moo metra*	measure me
που είναι ο καθρέφτης;	*poo ine o kathreftis?*	Where is the mirror?
δεν μου πάει καλά.	*ТНen moo pai kala.*	It doesn't suit me.
δεν μου κάνει.	*ТНen moo kani.*	It doesn't fit me.
είναι πολύ κοντό.	*ine poli kondo.*	It's too short.
μακρύ.	*makri.*	long.
φαρδύ.	*farthi.*	loose.
Έχετε το ίδιο σε . . .	*ehete to ітнio se . . .*	Do you have the same in . . . ?
ένα ζευγάρι παπούτσια	*ena zevgari papootsia*	pair of shoes
θα προτιμούσα . . .	*tha protimoosa . . .*	I'd rather have/prefer . . .
έκπτωσις	*ekptosis*	sales
η τιμή	*i timi*	price
Μου κάνετε μία έκπτωση;	*moo kanete mia ekptosi?*	Can you give me a discount?

See Topic Vocabulary for items of clothing, colors, etc.

Sizes for clothing and shoes

Shoes are a good buy in Greece, but it should be noted that the fit may be a little more generous in Greek sizes than the equivalent size in the United States.

Dresses							
USA	8	10	12	14	16	18	
Greece	36	38	40	42	44	46	
Suits/jackets/coats							
USA	36	38	40	42	44	46	
Greece	46	48	50	52	54	56	
Collar							
USA	13	13-1/2	14	14-1/2	15	15-1/2	16	16-1/2
Greece	33	34	35	37	38	39	41	42
Shoes							
USA	4-1/2	5-1/2	6-1/2	7-1/2	8-1/2	9-1/2	10-1/2	11-1/2
Greece	36	37	38	39/40	41	42	43	44

▶▶▶ **The newsstand** (περίπτερο *periptero*) in Greece is a vital part of everyday life, where you can make phone calls, buy newspapers and magazines, and get virtually all those little essentials you run out of late at night! Go there for postcards, candy, matches, cigarettes, sunglasses – the list is endless.

Μου δίνετε και την Athens News;
Give me the Athens News as well

Anne and Yiannis Vazakas are walking in Syntagma Square - Anne decides to buy an English newspaper.

Anne: **Θα ήθελα να μάθω τα νέα της Αγγλίας. Που μπορώ να βρώ**
tha ithela na matho ta nea tis Anglias. Poo boro na vro
αγγλικές εφημερίδες;
anglikes efimeriThes?

Yiannis: Είναι πολύ εύκολο. Υπάρχουν παντού περίπτερα που μπορείς
ine poli efkolo. iparhoon pandoo periptera, poo boris
να αγοράσεις ό,τι θέλεις.
na agorasis oti thelis.

Anne: Θα ήθελα την εφημερίδα "Guardian." Την έχετε;
(going up to a newsstand) tha ithela tin efimeriTHa
Guardian. tin ehete?

Owner: Λυπάμαι, όχι αλλά κοιτάξτε στο πλάι. Πρέπει να είναι εκεί
lipame, ohi, ala kitakste sto plai. prepi na ine eki
οι "Times" και η "Daily Mail"
i Times ke i Daily Mail.

Anne: Α, ναι, εδώ είναι οι "Times".
a, ne, eTHo ine i Times.

Yiannis: Ξέρεις Αννν, στην Ελλάδα υπάρχει η εφημερίδα "Athens News"
kseris, Anne, stin ellaTHa iparhi i efimeriTHa Athens
News
στα αγγλικά.
sta anglika.

Anne: Μου δίνετε και την "Athens News";
(to newsstand owner) moo THinete ke tin Athens News?

Phrases from the dialogue

Θα ήθελα . . .	tha ithela . . .	I'd like . . .
να μάθω	na matho	to learn
Που μπορώ να βρω . . .	poo boro na vro . . .	?Where can I find . . . ?
η εφημερίδα	i efimeriTHa	newspaper
εύκολο	efkolo	easy
παντού	pandoo	everywhere
που μπορείς να αγοράσεις	poo boris na agorasis	where you can buy
ό,τι θέλεις	oti thelis	whatever you like
λυπάμαι	lipame	I'm sorry
κοιτάξτε	kitakste	look (imperative)
πρέπει να είναι	prepi na ine	it must be
στο πλάι	sto plai	at the side

Newsstand items

πούρο	pouro	cigar
πακέτο τσιγάρα	paketto tsigara	pack of cigarettes
σοκολάτα	sokolata	chocolate bar
φιλμ: φωτογραφίες (n.)	film: fotografies	film: prints
σλάιντς	slides	slides
είκοσι τέσσερις	ikosi tesseris	24 (exposures)
τριάντα έξη	trianda eksi	36 (exposures)
οδηγός	oTHigos	guidebook
αναπτήρας	anaptiras	lighter
χάρτης	hartis	map
περιοδικό	perioTHiko	magazine
κουτί σπίρτα	kouti spirta	box of matches
αγγλική εφημερίδα	angliki efimeriTHa	English newspaper
κάρτα	karta	postcard
στυλό	stilo	pen
γυαλιά ηλίου	yalia iliou	sunglasses
καραμέλλες	karamelles	candy

the way it works
How to say "I need"

So far you've met groups of verbs ending in -ω -o, e.g., θέλω thelo, and
-αω -ao, e.g., μιλάω milao.

On page 56, Peter uses the verb χρειάζομαι hriazome, I need. This verb
belongs to another group of Greek verbs, ending in -ομαι -ome. This is
how it conjugates:

χρειάζομαι	hriazome	I need
χρειάζεσαι	hriazese	you need (sing.)
χρειάζεται	hriazete	he/she needs
χρειαζόμαστε	hriazomaste	we need
χρειάζεστε	hriazeste	you need (plural)
χρειάζονται	hriazonde	they need

I can, I must

As you saw in the last unit, **θέλω να** *thelo na*, I want, is usually followed by a different form of the verb. There are two other important verbs in Greek that have the same construction, **μπορώ να** *boro na*, I can, and **πρέπει να** *prepi na*, I must. Here is the conjugation for **μπορώ** *boro*:

μπορώ να φύγω	*boro na figo*	I can leave
μπορείς να φύγεις	*boris na fiyis*	you can leave
μπορεί να φύγει	*bori na fiyi*	he can leave
μπορούμε να φύγουμε	*boroome na figoome*	we can leave
μπορείτε να φύγετε	*borite na fiyete*	you can leave
μπορούν(ε) να φύγουνε	*boroon(e) na figoon*	they can leave

Notice how *both* verbs change their endings.

πρέπει να *prepi na*, I must, however, is an impersonal verb and stays the same in all persons. Only the verb that follows changes its endings:

πρέπει να πάω	*prepi na pao*	I must go
πρέπει να πας	*prepi na pas*	you must go
πρέπει να πάει	*prepi na pai*	he must go
πρέπει να πάμε	*prepi na pame*	we must go
πρέπει να πάτε	*prepi na pate*	you must go
πρέπει να πάνε	*prepi na pane*	they must go

See page 66 for the future forms of other common verbs which are used after **μπορώ να** *boro na* and **πρέπει να** *prepi na*.

things to do

4.4   Complete this dialogue in a shoe store:

You: (Do you have these shoes in my size?)
Assistant: **Τι μέγεθος είστε κυρία;**
             ti megethos iste, kiria?
You: (In England I'm size 6. What's that in Greece?)
Assistant: **Είναι τριάντα εννέα.**
             ine trianda ennea.
You: (I like the blue ones)
Assistant: **Τα μπλε, μέγεθος τριάντα εννέα – Ένα λεπτό κυρία.**
             ta ble, megethos trianda ennea – ena lepto, kiria.
You: (They are a little large – can I try size 38?)
Assistant: **Λυπάμαι, δεν έχουμε. Τα έχω σε καφέ.**
             lipame, THen ehoume. Ta eho se kafe.
You: (OK, I'll take the brown, size 38)

4.5   Ask where/if you can do the following:

1   Can I see the menu, please?
2   Can we have a table for four, please?
3   Where can I find a pharmacy?
4   Can I try on this dress, please?

EXCURSIONS

Sea travel Piraeus is the main port of Athens. Ships leave from there for the islands in the Saronic and Aegean. The hydrofoils (**ιπτάμενο** *iptameno*), or Flying Dolphins, offer a fast service to the near islands of Aegina, Poros, Hydra, and Spetses, for example, and leave from their own moorings at Marina Zea in Piraeus. You can also go by Flying Dolphin to the islands of the Sporades, Skiathos, Skopelos, and Alonisos – leaving from Agios Konstantinos and Volos. Hydrofoil tickets should be reserved in advance during the peak tourist season from the office in Syntagma Square, or through travel agents.

Με το πλοίο για τη Μύκονο
By boat to Mikonos

Peter, Maria, and Costas decide to take a boat trip to another island to get a change of scenery.

Peter: Πόση ώρα κάνει το πλοίο για τη Μύκονο;
        possi ora kani to plio ya ti Mikono?
Costas: Τρείς ώρες περίπου.
        tris ores peripoo.
Peter: Σταματάει σε άλλα νησιά;
        stamatai se alla nisia?
Costas: Στη Δήλο για μία ώρα. Πρέπει να αγοράσουμε τα εισιτήρια
        sti тнilo, ya mia ora. prepi na agorassoome ta isitiria
        αμέσως, γιατί έχει πάντα πολύ κόσμο.
        amesos, yati ehi panda poli kosmo.

Maria: Τι θέση θα ταξιδέψουμε;
         ti thesi tha taksiΤΗepsoome?
Costas: Τουριστική γιατί είναι πιο φτηνή.
         tooristiki yati ine pyo ftini.
Peter: Τι καιρό θα έχουμε;
         ti kero tha ehoome?
Maria: Θα έχουμε λίγο θάλασσα. Μήπως παθαίνεις ναυτία, Peter;
         tha ehoome ligo thalassa. mipos pathenis naftia, Peter?
Peter: Μέχρι τώρα όχι, αλλά δεν ταξιδεύω με πλοίο συχνά.
         mehri tora ohi, alla ΤΗen taksiΤΗevo me plio sihna.

Words and Phrases from the dialogue

Πόση ώρα κάνει το πλοίο;	*posi ora kani to plio?*	How long does the boat take?
περίπου	*peripoo*	about
Σταματάει;	*stamatai?*	Does it stop?
σε άλλα νησιά	*se alla nisia*	at other islands
πρέπει να -ουμε . . .	*prepi na -oome . . .*	we must . . .
αμέσως	*amesos*	right away
γιατί	*yati*	because
πολύς κόσμος	*polis kosmos*	a lot of people
πάντα	*panda*	always
τι θέση	*ti thesi*	what seat (i.e. what class)?
θα ταξιδέψουμε;	*tha taksiΤΗepsoome?*	shall we travel?
τι καιρό θα έχουμε;	*ti kero tha ehoome?*	What weather will we have?
μήπως	*mipos*	perhaps
παθαίνω ναυτία	*patheno naftia*	I suffer from seasickness
μέχρι τώρα	*mehri tora*	until now
με πλοίο	*me plio*	by boat
συχνά	*sihna*	often/frequently

Other useful words and phrases

Που βγάζουνε εισιτήρια;	*poo vgazoone isitiria?*	Where do they issue tickets?
το πρακτορίο	*to praktorio*	ticket office/agency
πληροφορίες	*plirofories*	information
το ταξίδι	*to taksiΤΗi*	journey
το φέρρυ-μποτ	*to ferri bot*	ferry boat
η καμπίνα	*i kabina*	cabin
πρώτη θέση	*proti thesi*	first-class seats
το κατάστρωμα	*to katastroma*	deck
το λιμάνι	*to limani*	harbor
η παραλία	*i paralia*	coast/seashore

Με το πούλμαν για τους Δελφούς
By bus to Delphi

Anne has agreed to meet Mr. and Mrs. Vazakas, and go with them on a day trip to Delphi – the site of the ancient oracle.

Yiannis: Να η Ανν. Έρχεται!
na i Anne. erhete!

Eleni: Γειά σου Ανν Είσαι στην ώρα σου όπως όλοι οι Άγγλοι.
ya soo Anne. ise stin ora soo opos oli i angli.

Anne: Γειά σας. **Τι ωραίος καιρός σήμερα!**
ya sas. ti oreos keros simera!

Yiannis: Το λεωφορείο φεύγει στις οκτώμιση και φτάνει στους
to leoforio fevyi stis oktomisi ke ftani stoos
Δελφούς στις εντεκάμιση.
THelfous stis endekamisi.

Anne: **Ωραία. Τι θα δούμε στους Δελφούς;**
orea. ti tha THoome stoos THelfoos?

Yiannis: Θα δούμε το Μουσείο, το Στάδιο και το Μαντείο.
tha THoome to moosio, to statHio ke to mandio.

Anne: Πόσες ώρες θα μείνουμε εκεί;
posses ores tha meenoome eki?

Eleni: Τέσσερις-πέντε. Το βράδυ θα έρθεις στο σπίτι μας
tesseris-pende. to vratHi tha erthis sto spiti mas
να φάμε μαζί.
na fame mazi.

Anne: Ευχαριστώ πολύ. Η ελληνική φιλοξενία είναι φημισμένη
παντού!
efharisto poli. i elliniki filoksenia ine fimismeni pandoo!

63

Words and phrases from the dialogue

η Ανν έρχεται	*i Anne erhete*	Anne is coming
στην ώρα	*stin ora*	on time
όπως όλοι οι Άγγλοι	*opos oli i Angli*	like all the English
Τι ωραίος καιρός!	*ti oreos keros!*	What lovely weather!
σήμερα	*simera*	today
στους Δελφούς	*stoos THelfoos*	at Delphi
Τι θα δούμε;	*ti tha THoome?*	What will we see?
το Στάδιο	*o staTHio*	stadium
το Μαντείο	*to Mandio*	Oracle
θα μείνουμε	*tha meenoome*	we will stay
το βράδυ	*to vraTHi*	in the evening
θα έρθεις στο σπίτι μας	*tha erthis sto spiti mas*	you'll come to our house
να φάμε μαζί	*na fame mazi*	for us to eat together
η φιλοξενία	*i filoksenia*	hospitality
φημισμένος,η,ο	*fimismenos -i -o*	famous
παντού	*pandoo*	everywhere

Other useful words and phrases

με το πούλμαν	*me to poolman*	by coach
η εκδρομή	*i ekTHromi*	trip/excursion
ο συνοδός	*o sinoTHos*	courier
ο ξεναγός	*o ksenagos*	guide
ο οδηγός	*o oTHigos*	driver
αποσκευές	*aposkeves*	luggage
Αυτή είναι η θέση μου.	*afti ine i thesi moo.*	This is my seat.
Πού θα σταματήσουμε;	*poo tha stamatisoome?*	Where will we stop?

Vocabulary of Ancient Greece

η αγορά	*i agora*	ancient marketplace
το αμφιθέατρο	*to amfitheatro*	amphitheater
ο ναός	*o naos*	temple
η κολώνα	*i kolona*	column
τα ερείπια	*ta eripia*	ruins

Καλώς ώρισες στο σπίτι μας
Welcome to our house

Anne and her Greek friends have had a wonderful day out, and have now returned to the Vazakas' house in Pagrati.

Eleni: **Καλώς ώρισες στο σπίτι μας**, Ανν.
kalos orises sto spiti mas, Anne.

Anne: **Καλώς σας βρήκα.** Κάτι τέτοιο λέτε, έτσι δεν είναι;
kalos sas vrika. kati tetio lete, etsi THen ine?

Yiannis: Anne, έγινες πραγματική Ελληνίδα. Πέρασε στη βεράντα –
Anne, eyines pragmatiki ellini THa. perase sti veranda –
τι θα πάρεις;
ti tha paris?

Anne: Λίγο κρασί άσπρο με σόδα, ευχαριστώ.
ligo krasi aspro me soTHa, efharisto.

Yiannis: **Πώς περνάς στις διακοπές;**
pos pernas stis THiakopes?

Anne: **Περνάω πολύ ωραία. Διασκεδάζω πολύ. Ευχαριστώ πολύ για**
pernao poli orea. THiaskeTHazo poli. efharisto poli ya
την πρόσκληση. Το σπίτι σας είναι θαυμάσιο. Μένετε εδώ
tin prosklisi. to spiti sas ine thavmasio. menete eTHo
πολύ καιρό;
poli kero?

Eleni: Μένουμε εδώ δέκα χρόνια. Είναι πολύ κοντά στο κέντρο και
menoome eTHo THeka hronya. ine poli konda sto kendro ke
βλέπουμε την
vlepoome tin
Ακρόπολη.
Akropoli.

Anne: **Τι όμορφη θέα!**
ti omorfi thea!

Yiannis: Τι θα κάνεις το
ti tha kanis to
Σαββατοκύριακο;
savvatokiriako?
Πάμε στα μπουζούκια;
pame sta boozookia?

Words and phrases from the dialogue

κάλως ωρίσατε	*kalos orisate*	welcome
καλώς σας βρήκα	*kalos sas vrika*	I'm glad to be here
		(= I've found you well)
κάτι τέτοιο λέτε	*kati tetio lete*	you say something like that
έτσι δεν είναι;	*etsi THen ine?*	isn't it?/don't you?, etc.
έγινες	*eyines*	you've become
πέρασε	*perase*	pass through (imperative)
Τι θα πάρεις;	*ti tha paris?*	What will you have/drink?
Πως περνάς;	*pos pernas?*	How are you spending your time?

στις διακοπές	stis diakopes	on vacation
Περνάω πολύ ωραία.	pernao poli orea.	I'm having a good time.
διασκεδάζω	thiaskeΤΗazo	I'm enjoying myself
η πρόσκληση	i prosklisi	invitation
θαυμάσιος -α -ο	thavmasios-a-o	wonderful
πολύ καιρό	poli kero	a long time
βλέπουμε	vlepoome	we see/we can see
Τι όμορφη θέα	ti omorfi thea	What a beautiful view!
το Σαββατοκύριακο	to savvatokiriako	the weekend
στα μπουζούκια	sta boozookia	to a bouzouki place

Other useful words and phrases

το διαμέρισμα	to thiamerisma	apartment
το μπαλκόνι	to balkoni	the balcony
Πως είναι το σπίτι;	pos ine to spiti?	What's your house like?
Που μένετε;	poo menete?	Where do you live?
καθίστε	kathiste	sit down/take a seat
Καπνίζετε;	kapnizete?	Do you smoke?
(δεν) καπνίζω	(ΤΗen) kapnizo	I (don't) smoke

the way it works

Future tense

To form the future (e.g., I'll go) put the word θα *tha* before the verb. There are some verbs which keep their normal present tense form after θα *tha*— e.g., κάνω *kano* θα κάνω *tha kano* (I'll do/make); περιμένω *perimeno* θα περιμένω *tha perimeno* (I'll wait).

More verbs, however, change their form after θα *tha*. Here are the most important:

Present		Future		
πηγαίνω	piyeno	θα πάω	tha pao	I'll go
στέλνω	stelno	θα στείλω	tha stilo	I'll send
παίρνω	perno	θα πάρω	tha paro	I'll take
μένω	meno	θα μείνω	tha mino	I'll stay
αγοράζω	agorazo	θα αγοράσω	tha agoraso	I'll buy
τηλεφωνώ	tilefono	θα τηλεφωνήσω	tha tilefonisso	I'll phone
νοικιάζω	nikiazo	θα νοικιάσω	tha nikiaso	I'll rent
χαλάω	halao	θα χαλάσω	tha halasso	I'll change
λέω	leo	θα πω	tha po	I'll say
βλέπω	vlepo	θα δω	tha ΤΗΟ	I'll see

Some examples:

Θα πάμε στην Ελλάδα του χρόνου.
tha pame stin ellaΤΗa too hronoo.

We'll go to Greece next year.

Η Μαρία θα στείλει μια κάρτα στην μητέρα της.
i Maria tha stili mia karta sti mitera tis.

Maria will send a postcard to her mother.

Orders and instructions (con)

On Wednesday you learned about the plural/polite imperative form.

In the last dialogue Yiannis asks Anne to pass through to the veranda. As he knows her quite well now, he uses πέρασε *perase,* which is the singular familiar form of the imperative. Here is a list of common verbs, showing the form.

First person present		Familiar imperative		
φέρνω	ferno	φέρε	fere	bring
πηγαίνω	piyeno	πήγαινε	piyene	go
δίνω	THino	δώσε	those	give
έρχομαι	erhome	έλα	ela	come
κάθομαι	kathome	κάθισε	kathise	sit
παίρνω	perno	πάρε	pare	take
περιμένω	perimeno	περίμενε	perimene	wait
αφήνω	afino	άφησε	afise	leave
λέω	leo	πες	pes	say
στρίβω	strivo	στρίψε	stripse	turn
περνάω	pernao	πέρασε	perase	pass
δοκιμάζω	THOkimazo	δοκίμασε	THOkimase	try

things to do

5.1   The details of your excursion haven't been announced yet, so:

1   Ask what time the boat leaves.
2   Ask how much the ticket is.
3   Ask how long the trip lasts.
4   Ask when the boat returns.
5   Ask where you'll have lunch.
6   Ask if you must buy tickets now.

5.2   You've found a seat next to a Greek person on a bus. Complete the dialogue:

You: (Ask if the seat is free)
Greek: **Ναι καθίστε. Πηγαίνετε στη Βουλιαγμένη;**
You: (Say no – you have to get off at Glyfada)
Greek: **Ξέρετε που πρέπει να κατεβείτε;**
You: (No, you're not sure – ask if he/she can tell you where)
Greek: **Ασφαλώς- Είστε εδώ για διακοπές;**
You: (Yes, but you'll be leaving in two days)

ENTERTAINMENT

With such wonderful sea, landscape, food, drink, and people, all life is entertainment in Greece!

Greeks like to eat out in the evenings, usually well after 9:00 pm, and go on into the small hours. Discos and cocktail bars are plentiful and fashionable in the islands – in Athens you'll need to ask your hotel to recommend night clubs and discos to suit your taste and pocket.

In the summer months movie theaters are in the open air. Most films are imported and always shown with their original soundtrack and Greek subtitles – so you won't miss out on new releases.

For a traditional Greek evening out, you can go to a bouzouki place, where you'll hear traditional Greek songs accompanied by the mandolin-like bouzouki, which gives Greek music its distinctive sound, and often Greek dancing. Bouzouki places can be quite expensive, so check first – you may also have to make reservations. Remember, things get going quite late, so don't show up at 7:00 pm!

In Athens you can attend classical music concerts at the Herod Atticus Theater at the foot of the Acropolis. See the publication *The Athenian* for weekly events or a copy of *Athens News* (daily except Mondays), an English-language newspaper available from central newsstands in Athens. This gives details of all events, concerts, and films.

Θέλω τρία εισιτήρια για αύριο
Three tickets for tomorrow, please

Anne wants some tickets for a play.

Anne: Θέλω τρία εισιτήρια για αύριο. Πρέπει να τα κλείσω τώρα, η
thelo tria isitiria ya avrio. Prepi na ta kliso tora, i
μπορώ να τα αγοράσω πριν την παράσταση;
boro na ta agorasso prin tin parastasi?

Clerk: Θα έχει πολύ κόσμο. Πρέπει να κλείσετε θέσεις τώρα.
tha ehi poli kosmo. prepi na klisete thesis tora.

Anne: Εντάξει. Θέλω τρεις θέσεις στην πλατεία για τη βραδυνή
endaksi. thelo tris thesis stin platia gia ti vraтнini.
παράσταση. Τι ώρα αρχίζει;
parastasi. Ti ora arhizi?

Clerk: Στις εννιά. Λοιπόν έχω τρείς πολύ καλές θέσεις στην τρίτη
stis ennya. lipon, eho tris poli kales thesis stin triti
σειρά. Κοστίζουν οκτακόσιες δραχμές η κάθε μία. Δύο
sira. kostizoon oktakosies тнrahmes i kathe mia.   тнio
χιλιάδες τετρακόσιες δραχμές.
hiliaтнes tetrakosies тнrahmes.

Anne: Ευχαριστώ για τη βοήθεια.
efharisto ya ti voithia.

Words and phrases from the dialogue

για αύριο	*ya avrio*	for tomorrow
Πρέπει να τα κλείσω;	*prepi na ta kliso?*	Do I have to reserve them?
ή μπορώ να τα αγοράσω;	*i boro na ta agorasso?*	or can I buy them?
πριν την παράσταση	*prin tin parastasi*	before the performance
πρέπει να κλείσετε	*prepi na klisete*	you must make reservations
τρεις θέσεις στην πλατεία	*tris thesis stin platia*	3 seats in the stalls
βραδινή παράσταση	*vraтнini parastasi*	evening performance
στην τρίτη σειρά	*stin triti sira*	in the third row
για την βοήθεια	*ya tin voithia*	for (your) help

Other useful words and phrases

Going to the movies or theater

το σινεμά	*to sinema*	movie theater
το έργο/φίλμ	*to ergo/film*	film (also η ταινία/*i tenia*)
το πρόγραμμα	*to programma*	program

Είναι το φίλμ στα Αγγλικά; *ine to film sta anglika?* Is the film in English?

Η απογευματινή/βραδινή παράσταση	afternoon/evening performance
i apoyevmatini/vraтнini parastasi	
το διάλειμμα	intermission
to тнialima	
Τι παίζει στο σινεμά;	What's playing at the movie theater?
ti pezi sto sinema?	

Τι ώρα αρχίζει/τελειώνει; *ti ora arhizi/telioni?*
What time does it begin/end?

η συναυλία	*i sinavlia*	concert
το θέατρο	*to theatro*	theater
το έργο	*to ergo*	play
η πλατεία	*i platia*	stalls
ο εξώστης	*o eksostis*	balcony

Θέλω να κλείσω δυο εισιτήρια για . . . I want to reserve two tickets for . . .
thelo na kliso тнio isitiria ya . . .

το αστυνομικό	*to astinomiko*	detective (film)
η κωμωδία	*i komoтнia*	comedy
το δράμα	*to тнrama*	drama
το μουσικοχορευτικό	*to moosikohoreftiko*	musical

Going out on the town

Πρέπει να κλείσουμε	*prepi na klisoome*	Do we have to reserve
ένα τραπέζι;	*ena trapezi?*	a table?
η ντίσκο	*i disko*	discotheque
το ναΐτκλάμπ	*to naitklab*	nightclub
το κέντρο	*to kendro*	bouzouki place
Πάμε στα μπουζούκια;	*pame sta boozookia?*	Shall we go to a bouzouki place?
Πάμε για χορό;	*pame ya horo?*	Shall we go dancing?

Θέλω να νοικιάσω ένα ποδήλατο θάλασσας
I want to rent a pedal boat

Peter wants to rent a pedal boat for an hour or so.

Peter: **Θέλω να νοικιάσω ένα ποδήλατο θάλασσας για μια ώρα.**
thelo na nikiaso ena poтнilato thalassas ya mia ora.
Πόσο κάνει;
Posso kani?

Boy: Τριακόσιες δραχμές η μια ώρα – πεντακόσιες για δύο ώρες.
Triakosies тнrahmes i mia ora – pendakosies ya тнio ores.

Peter: **Νομίζω μια ώρα είναι αρκετά.**
Nomizo mia ora ine arketa.

Boy: Εντάξει. Αλλά δεν πρέπει να πάτε περα από τις σημαδούρες.
Endaksi. alla THEN prepi na pate pera apo tis simaTHoores.

Peter: Μήπως υπάρχουν καρχαρίες πιο έξω;
(laughingly) *mipos iparhoon karharies pyo ekso?*

Useful words and phrases from the dialogue

θέλω να νοικιάσω	*thelo na nikiaso*	I want to rent
ένα ποδήλατο θάλασσας	*ena poTHilato thalassas*	pedal boat
για μια ώρα	*ya mia ora*	for an hour
νομίζω	*nomizo*	I think
είναι αρκετά	*ine arketa*	it is enough
δεν πρέπει να πάτε	*THEN prepi na pate*	you mustn't go
πέρα απο τις σημαδούρες	*pera apo tis simaTHoores*	beyond the buoys
καρχαρίες	*karharies*	sharks
πιο έξω	*pyo ekso*	farther out

Other useful words and phrases

On the beach

ΑΠΑΓΟΡΕΥΕΤΑΙ ΤΟ ΚΟΛΥΜΠΙ!   swimming prohibited!
apagorevete to kolimbi!
Πως είναι η πλαζ – έχει άμμο ή πέτρες;   How's the beach – sand or pebbles?
pos ine i plaz – ehi ammo i petres?
Είναι η θάλασσα επικίνδυνη εδώ;   Is the sea dangerous here?
ine i thalassa epikinTHini eTHO?

Υπάρχει ακτοφύλακας;	*iparhi aktofilakas?*	Is there a lifeguard?
Υπάρχουν ρεύματα;	*iparhoon revmata?*	Are there currents?
το στρώμα θάλασσας	*to stroma thalassas*	air mattress
η καμπίνα	*i kambina*	cabin
η τέντα	*i tenda*	sunshade
η ομπρέλλα	*i ombrella*	umbrella
Μπορώ να νοικιάσω;	*boro na nikiaso . . . ?*	Can I rent?
Πως λέτε **surfboard** στα Ελληνικά;	*pos lete surfboard sta Ellinika?*	What is surfboard in Greek?

71

Camping

το κάμπινγκ	*to kamping*	campsite
η κατασκήνωση	*i kataskinosi*	campsite
η σκηνή	*i skini*	tent
το τροχόσπιτο	*to trohospito*	caravan/trailer

Που μπορούμε να κατασκηνώσουμε τη νύχτα; Where can we camp for the night?
poo boroome na kataskinosoome ti nihta?

Μπορούμε να ανάψουμε φωτιά; Can we light a fire?
boroome na anapsoome fotia?

Το νερό – είναι πόσιμο; Is the water drinkable?
to nero – ine posimo?

Υπάρχουν ντους/λουτρά/τουαλέττες; Are there showers/baths/toilets?
iparhoon doos/lootra/tooalletes?

things to do

5.3 You want to buy tickets for a play:

1 Ask if there are seats for this evening.
2 Ask how much the tickets are.
3 Say you want four tickets.
4 Ask how much that is altogether.
5 Ask what time the performance starts and finishes.

ΚΕΑ (Υπερείδου 21, Πλάκα, τηλ. 3229889): "Άσπρο - μαύρο", μονόπρακτα των Όσκαρ Γουάιλντ, Γκέλντεργόντ, Μπέλλου.
ΚΕΡΚΙΔΑ (Σοφούλη 31, θύρα 10 γηπέδου Πανιωνίου, τηλ. 9349560). "Το φιντανάκι" του Π. Χορν - Νότα Παρούση, Τάκης Σταμάτατος.

ΦΛΟΡΙΝΤΑ (Μετσόβου 4 και Πατησίων, τηλ.: 8228501) Γ. Κατσαμπή: Ένα κορίτσι στη ... μπανιέρα μου". Κ. Παπανίκα - Θ, Κατσαδράμης, κ. ά.
ΘΕΑΤΡΟ ΔΟΡΑΣ ΣΤΡΑΤΟΥ (Λόφος φιλοππάπου): "Ελληνικοί χοροί".

5.4 You want to organize something for the evening and ask the hotel receptionist:

You: (Ask what's playing at the movie theater tonight)
Receptionist: Παίζει μία ελληνική ταινία.
You: (Ask what else you can do)
Receptionist: Πρέπει να πάτε στα μπουζούκια.
You: (Ask if you have to reserve a table)
Receptionist: Ναι, νομίζω, θέλετε να τηλεφωνήσω;
You: (Say yes – ask for a table for two at 9:30)

▶ **Renting a car/motorbike** Cars cost a great deal more in Greece than other European countries, so car rental is more expensive too. It's worth it, though, to get out into the countryside, or to find secluded beaches.

Most car rental agencies in Athens are situated at the top of Syngrou Avenue, opposite Hadrian's Gate. Your hotel can also arrange car rentals. You'll need a current driver's license, of course, and your passport. It is advisable, although expensive, to take out full collision protection – Greeks are enthusiastic and boisterous drivers, who give no quarter to cautious drivers!

On the islands there are many small car and motorcycle rental businesses. Motorbikes are convenient for getting around cheaply, especially on a bigger island, but be very careful at night on small roads – a lot of accidents happen.

Θέλω να νοικιάσω ένα αυτοκίνητο
I want to rent a car

Peter, Costas, and Maria want to rent a car for the day.

Costas: **Θέλω να νοικιάσω ένα αυτοκίνητο.** Το πιο μικρό που έχετε.
thelo na nikiaso ena aftokinito – to pyo mikro poo ehete.

Assistant: **Τι μάρκα θέλετε;**
ti marka thelete?

Costas: Ένα Φίατ με δύο πόρτες.
ena Fiat me THio portes.

Assistant: Εντάξει. Για πόσες μέρες το θέλετε;
endaksi. ya posses meres to thelete?

Maria: Μόνο για μία ημέρα.
monoya mia mera.

Costas: **Πόσο κάνει μαζί με την ασφάλεια;**
posso kani mazi me tin asfalia?

Assistant: Τέσσερις χιλιάδες το αυτοκίνητο, χίλιες η ασφάλεια.
tesseris hiliaTHes to aftokinito, hilies i asfalia.
Επιπλέον, τριάντα δραχμές κατά χιλιόμετρο. Πρέπει να
epipleon, trianda THrahmes kata hiliometro. prepi na
πληρώσετε μία προκαταβολή. **Μπορώ να δω την άδεια**
plirosete mia prokatavoli. boro na THo tin aTHia
οδηγήσεώς σας, παρακαλώ;
στηiyiseos sas, parakalo?

Costas: Ορίστε. Είναι καθαρή!
oriste. ine kathari!

Words and phrases from the dialogue

θέλω να νοικιάσω	thelo na nikiaso	I want to rent
το αυτοκίνητο	to aftokinito	car
το πιο μικρό	to pyo mikro	the smallest
με δύο πόρτες	me THio portes	with 2 doors
η ασφάλεια	i asfalia	insurance
επιπλέον	epipleon	on top of that
κατά χιλιόμετρο	kata hiliometro	per kilometer
πρέπει να πληρώσετε	prepi na plirosete	you must pay
η προκαταβολή	i prokatavoli	deposit
η άδεια οδηγήσεως	i aTHia oTHiyiseos	driver's license
καθαρός -η -ο	katharos -i -o	clean

Other useful words and phrases

αυτόματο	*aftomato*	automatic (transmission)
Έχει ραδιόφωνο	*ehi raTHiofono*	it has a radio
κασσετόφωνο	*kassetofono*	cassette player
μπορώ να αφήσω το	*boro na afiso to*	Can I leave the
αυτοκίνητο στον/στην	*aftokinito ston/stin . . .*	car in . . . ?
με ελεύθερα χιλιόμετρα	*me elefthera hiliometra*	with unlimited kms
ημερήσια χρέωση	*imerisia hreosi*	daily charge
εβδομαδιαία χρέωση	*evTHomathiea hreosi*	weekly charge
φόροι	*fori*	taxes
η παράδοση	*i paraTHosi*	delivery
η παραλαβή	*i paralavi*	collection
η πλήρης ασφάλεια	*i pliris asfalia*	full insurance

Road signs

ΑΔΙΕΞΟΔΟΣ	*aTHieksoTHos*	no through road
ΑΠΑΓΟΡΕΥΕΤΑΙ	*apagorevete*	no
Η ΕΙΣΟΔΟΣ	*i isoTHos*	entry
Η ΣΤΑΘΜΕΥΣΗ	*i stathmefsi*	parking
ΤΟ ΠΡΟΣΠΕΡΑΣΜΑ	*to prosperasma*	passing
Η ΑΝΑΜΟΝΗ	*i anamoni*	standing
ΔΗΜΟΣΙΑ ΕΡΓΑ	*THimosia erga*	road works
ΚΙΝΔΥΝΟΣ/ΠΡΟΣΟΧΗ	*kinTHinos/prosohi*	caution
ΜΟΝΟΔΡΟΜΟΣ	*monoTHromos*	one-way street
ΠΑΡΑΚΑΜΠΤΗΡΙΟΣ	*parakamptirios*	detour
ΑΡΓΑ	*arga*	slow

Driving in Greece In town the speed limit is between 40 and 60 kph; on highways between 80 and 100 kph. Place names are signposted in Greek and Roman letters. The equivalent of the AAA is ELPA. ELPA also has tourist information offices in larger towns.

Gas is available in two grades – regular and premium.

Driving in Greece

On the road

οδηγείτε δεξιά	*oTHiyite THeksia*	keep right
η εθνική οδος	*i ethniki oTHos*	national highway
τα διόδια	*ta THioTHia* (plu.)	toll
η διασταύρωση	*i THiastavrosi*	junction
το φανάρι/τα φανάρια	*to fanari/ta fanaria*	traffic light/s
η κυκλοφορεία	*i kikloforia*	traffic
η ταχύτητα	*i tahitita*	speed
το όριο ταχύτητας	*to orio tahititas*	speed limit
το πάρκινγκ	*to parking*	parking lot
το παρκόμετρο	*to parkometro*	parking meter

At the gas station

το πρατήριο βενζίνης	to pratirio venzinis	gas station
η βενζίνη	i venzini	gas
απλή	apli	regular
σούπερ	sooper	premium
βάλτε μου βενζίνη για...	valte moo venzini ya . . .	Give me . . . drachmas
δραχμές.	THrahmes.	worth of gas.
γεμίστε το	yemiste to	fill it up
το λάδι	to laTHi	oil
ελέγξτε το λάδι	elengste to laTHi	check the oil
τα λάστιχα	ta lastiha	tires
η πίεση	i piesi	pressure
το ντίζελ	to dizel	diesel
το τροχόσπιτο	to trohospito	caravan

Asking the way

Πόσα χιλιόμετρα είναι μέχρι . . . ;
possa hiliometra ine mehri . . . ?
How many km is it to . . . ?

Μπορείτε να μου δείξετε το δρόμο για . . . ;
borite na moo THiksete to THromo ya . . . ?
Can you show me the way to . . . ?

Που οδηγεί αυτός ο δρόμος;
poo oTHiyi aftos o THromos?
Where does this road lead to . . . ?

Δείξτε μου που είμαι στον χάρτη.
THikste moo poo ime ston harti.
Show me where I am on the map.

Έχετε πάρει λάθος δρόμο.
ehete pari lathos THromo.
You've taken the wrong road.

things to do

6.1 You want to rent a car. Fill in the missing words in Greek:

You: (I want to rent) **ένα αυτοκίνητο** (with four doors).
Clerk: Τι μάρκα προτιμάτε;
You: **Θέλω** (a cheap car).
Clerk: Έχω ένα Opel Corsa.
You: (How much does it cost for 1 day?)
Clerk: Πέντε χιλιάδες δραχμές την ημέρα. Για πόσες μέρες το θέλετε;
You: (for three days)
Clerk: Μπορώ να δώ την άδεια οδηγήσεως;

6.2 You stop at a gas station:

1 Ask for a tankful of premium gas.
2 Ask for the oil to be checked.
3 Ask if the road goes to Athens.
4 Ask how many kilometers it is to Athens.

ACCIDENT AND EMERGENCY

έχει μια βλάβη/We've had a breakdown

Peter, Maria, and Costas are driving along the coast, looking for a place to swim. Suddenly the car stops. Costas goes to phone the car rental company.

Rental co.: Εμπρός;

Costas: Με λένε Κώστα Κιτάνο – νοικιάσαμε ένα αυτοκίνητο
me lene Kosta Kitano – nikiasame ena aftokinito
το πρωί – **τώρα έχει μία βλάβη.**
to proi – tora ehi mia vlavi.

Rental co.: **Τι έγινε, κύριε;**
ti eyine, kirie?

Costas: Ήτανε εντάξει στην αρχή, αλλά μετά σταμάτησε
itane endaksi stin arhi, alla meta stamatise
ξαφνικά και δεν ξεκινάει.
ksafnika ke ᴛнen keskinai.

Rental co.: Που είστε ακριβώς;
poo iste akrivos?

Costas: Περίπου πέντε χιλιόμετρα έξω από την πόλη.
peripoo pende hiliometra ekso apo tin poli.

Rental co.: Εντάξει, – υπάρχει ένα γκαράζ ένα χιλιόμετρο πιο κάτω στο
endaksi – iparhi ena garaz ena hiliometro pyo kato sto
δρόμο. Θα τους τηλεφωνήσω να στείλουν κάποιον να σας.
ᴛнromo. tha toos telefoniso na stiloon kapyon na sas
βοηθήσει.
voithisi.

Costas: Ευχαριστώ. Πέστε του να έρθει γρήγορα.
efharisto. peste too na erthi grigora.

Maria: Ήμουνα σίγουρη ότι θα είχαμε προβλήματα!
imoona sigoori oti tha ihame provlimata!

Useful words and phrases from the dialogue

εμπρός	embros	hello (answering phone)
με λένε	me lene	my name is
νοικιάσαμε	nikiasame	we rented
το πρωί	to proi	morning
Έχει μία βλάβη.	ehi mia vlavi.	We've had a breakdown.
Τι έγινε;	ti eyine?	What happened?
ήτανε εντάξει	itane endaksi	it was OK
στην αρχή	stin arhi	at the start/beginning
αλλά μετά	alla meta	but afterwards
η μηχανή	i mihani	the engine
σταμάτησε ξαφνικά	stamatise ksafnika	stopped suddenly
δεν ξεκινάει	THen ksekinai	it doesn't start
ακριβώς	akrivos	exactly
έξω από την πόλη	ekso apo tin poli	(5 km) outside the town
κάποιος -α- ο	kapios -ia -io	someone
να σας βοηθήσει	na sas voithisi	to help you
πέστε του	peste too	tell him
γρήγορα	grigora	quickly
ήμουνα σίγουρη	imoona sigoori	I was sure (fem.)

Problems with the car

το πλησιέστερο γκαράζ to plisiestero garaz	the nearest garage
ο γερανός o yeranos	tow truck
. . . δεν δουλεύει . . . THen THoolevi	the . . . isn't working
ο αριθμός κυκλοφορίας o arithmos kikloforias	license plate number
Μπορώ να χρησιμοποιήσω το τηλέφωνό σας; boro na hrisimopi-iso to tilefono sas?	Can I use your telephone?
Μπορείτε να με βοηθήσετε; borite na me voithisete?	Can you help me?
Τελείωσε η βενζίνη. teliose i venzini.	I've run out of gas.
Έπαθα μία βλάβη στο . . . epatha mia vlavi sto . . .	I've had a breakdown at . . .
Μπορείτε να στείλετε ένα μηχανικό; borite na stilete ena mihaniko?	Can you send a mechanic?
μπορείτε να επιδιορθώστε . . . ; borite na epiTHiorthosete . . . ?	Can you repair . . . ?
ο/η/το . . . είναι σπασμένος -η -ο o/i/to . . . ine spasmenos -i -o	the . . . is broken
έσκασε το λάστιχο. eskase to lastiho.	I have a flat tire.
Μπορείτε να αλλάξετε το λάστιχο; borite na allaksete to lastiho?	Can you change the tire?

For parts of the car, see topic vocabulary, page 97. General car travel phrases are on page 76.

USING THE TELEPHONE

Making phone calls in Greece You can find public phones at kiosks or other large establishments. Some of these phones take coins and others take special phone cards, which can be purchased at kiosks, post offices, or from an OTE (national phone service) office. Phone cards come in several different denominations.

If you don't plan on making enough calls to use an entire phone card, you can use a metered phone found at many kiosks. You pay after your call is completed. Local calls made this way are affordable, but long-distance calls can quickly become expensive.

You also can go to the OTE office (national phone service) to place both domestic and international calls. OTE offices can be found in most towns and are usually centrally located. When you arrive at the office, you will be assigned a private booth with a metered phone.

International calls made from a hotel can be subject to a large surcharge, so you can take advantage of phone offices or phone cards to save money when calling home. If you need to reach an operator who speaks English, you can reach one by dialing 161.

Some useful phone numbers

166 Ambulance
100 Police
171 Tourist police
199 Fire department

Telephone phrases

Με συνδέετε με . . .	*me sin*THΕ*ete me . . .*	Put me through to . . .
Θέλω να μιλήσω στον/στην . . .	*thelo na miliso ston/stin . . .*	I want to speak to . . .
Εμπρός - εδώ (Γιώργος)	*empros etho (yiorgos)*	Hello, (George) speaking . . .
πήρατε λάθος αριθμό	*pirate lathos arithmo*	wrong number
Πάρτε αργότερα.	*parte argotera.*	Call later.
δεν απαντάει	*THen apandai*	no answer
το τηλέφωνο δεν λειτουργεί	*to tilefono* THΕn *litooryi*	out of order
Σας ζητάνε στο τηλέφωνο.	*sas zitane sto tilefono.*	There's a call for you.
Μιλάει.	*milai.*	(The line is) busy.
		(lit. he/she is speaking)

Accidents Accidents can happen, so take care, especially when renting small motorcycles on the islands. Island roads are rarely lit at night, and the road surfaces can be uneven. Take care also when participating in water sports.

For most people the worst problems will be sunburn and stomachaches–not from the tap water, which is fine, but from overindulgence.

Greeks treat the midday sun (12–3 pm) with the greatest respect, so take their advice. Tan gradually, use a lotion with a high protection factor, and cover your head if no shade is available.

Greeks rarely drink alcohol without eating – not a bad rule to follow!

Health care in Greece As a matter of course, make sure you have good medical insurance before you leave. Few islands have full hospital emergency services. Private doctors and treatment can be expensive.

1 Police Emergency
2 Coast Guard Emergency
3 Duty Doctors (Athens-Pireus)
4 Emergency Hospitals
5 First Aid Center
6 Dental Emergency
7 Poison Center
8 Fire Department

ΤΗΛΕΦΩΝΑ ΑΝΑΓΚΗΣ

1	Άμεση Δράση Αστυνομίας ...	100
2	Άμεση Επέμβαση Λιμενικού.	108
3	Εφημ/ντες γιατροί Αθηνών..	
	Πειραιώς	105
4	Εφημερεύοντα νοσοκομεία...	106
5	Κέντρο άμεσης βοηθείας	166
6	Οδοντοιατρείο	6434001
7	Δηλητηριάσεων	779377
8	Πυροσβεστική	199

Useful words and phrases

(See Topic Vocabulary, pages 100–1, for parts of the body. Also Thursday for information and vocabulary on medicine and pharmacies.)

Δεν είμαι/αισθάνομαι καλά.	THEN ime/esthanome kala.	I don't feel well.
Είμαι άρρωστος -η.	ime arostos -i.	I'm ill.
Έπαθα δυστύχημα.	epatha THistihima.	I've had an accident.
Στραμπούλιξα τον αστράγαλο.	strabooliksa ton astragalo.	I've sprained my ankle.
έκαψα το/τη . . .	ekapsa to/ti . . .	I've burned my . . .
έκοψα το/τη . . .	ekopsa to/ti . . .	I've cut my . . .
Κόπηκα.	kopika.	I've cut myself.
με πονάει ο/η/το . . .	me ponai o/i/to . . .	my . . . hurts
Έχω ένα πόνο εδώ.	eho ena pono eTHo.	I have a pain here.
Έπεσα.	epesa.	I've fallen.
Είναι πρισμένο.	ine prismeno.	It's swollen.
Έχω πυρετό.	eho pireto.	I've got a temperature.
Έκανα μετό.	ekana meto.	I've been vomiting.
Είμαι καρδιακός/η	ime karthiakos/i.	I have a heart condition.
Έχασα τα χάπια μου	ehasa ta hapia moo.	I've lost my pills.
το φάρμακο	to farmako	medicine
Είμαι έγκυος	ime engios	I'm pregnant.
Είμαι διαβητικός -η.	ime thiavitikos -i.	I'm diabetic.
Με πονάει το δόντι μου.	me ponai to thondi moo.	I've got a toothache.
Παίρνω αντισυλλιπτικά χάπια.	perno andisilliptika hapia.	I'm on the pill.
Η γυναίκα μου περιμένει μωρό.	i yineka moo perimeni moro.	My wife is expecting a baby.
Είμαι αλλεργικός στην πενικιλλίνη.	ime alleryikos stin penikillini.	I'm allergic to penicillin.
νομίζω ότι ο/η/το . . . είναι σπασμένος,η,ο	nomizo oti o/i/to . . . ine spasmenos/i/o.	I think my . . . is broken.
Θέλω ένα γιατρό. οδοντίατρο.	thelo ena yatro orthondoyatro	I want a doctor. dentist.
Υπάρχει γιατρός στο/στη . . . ?	iparhi yatros sto/sti . . . ?	Is there a doctor in . . . ?
το ιατρείο	to iatrio	doctor's office
το νοσοκομείο	to nosokomio	hospital
Είναι επείγων.	ine epigon.	It's urgent.
Κάνετε γρήγορα.	kanete grigora.	Please hurry.
Χρειάζομαι ένα ασθενοφόρο.	hriazome ena asthenoforo.	I need an ambulance.
Χρειάζομαι ένα γιατρό που να μιλάει Αγγλικά.	hriazome ena yatro poo na milai anglika.	I need an English-speaking doctor.

Other emergencies

η αστυνομία	i astinomia	police
το αστυνομικό τμήμα	to astinomiko tmima	police station
η σύγκρουση	i singroosi	auto accident/crash
Τηλεφωνείστε στην αστυνομία αμέσως.	tilefoniste stin astinomia amesos.	Call the police immediately.

Θέλω ένα διερμηνέα.	thelo ena THierminea.	I want an interpreter.
Έχασα το πορτοφόλι μου.	ehasa to portofoli moo.	I've lost my wallet.
Χάθηκε το παιδί μου.	hathike to peTHi moo.	My child's lost.
Μου έκλεψαν το . . . μου.	moo eklepsan to . . .moo.	Someone's stolen my .
η πρεσβεία	i prezvia	embassy/consulate
η φωτιά	i fotia	fire
η πυροσβεστική αντλία	i pirosvestiki andlia	fire department
ο πυροσβέστης	o pirosvestis	fireman
Το δωμάτιο μου έπιασε φωτιά.	to THomatio moo epyase fotia.	My room is on fire.

ο ναυαγοσώστης	o navagosostis	lifeguard
Το παιδί μου δεν ξέρει κολύμπι.	to peTHi moo THen kseri kolimbi.	My child can't swim.
Βοήθεια	voithia	Help!
Πνίγεται.	pniyete.	He/She's drowning!

the way it works

Past tense

the past tense of the verb είμαι/ime, to be, is as follows:

ήμουν(α)	imoon(a)	I was
ήσουν(α)	isoon(a)	you were
ήταν(ε)	itan(e)	he/she/it was
ήμαστε	imaste	we were
ήσαστε	isaste	you were
ήταν(ε)	itan(e)	they were

The final (e) can be included or omitted.

The past tense of the verb έχω eho, I have, is as follows:

είχα	iha	I had
είχες	ihes	you had
είχε	ihe	he/she/it had
είχαμε	ihame	we had
είχατε	ihate	you had
είχαν(ε)	ihan(e)	they had

Ήμαστε στην Ελλάδα πέρυσι.
imaste stin ellaTHa perisi.
We were in Greece last year.

Ο Γιώργος δεν ήτανε στην ταβέρνα χθές.
o Yorgos THen itane stin taverna hthes.
George was not in the taverna yesterday.

Είχαμε ένα πρόβλημα με το αυτοκίνητο την περασμένη εβδομάδα.
ihame ena provlima me to aftokinito tin perasmeni evTHomaTHa.
We had a problem with the car last week.

Είχα πολλή δουλειά πριν τις διακοπές μου.
iha polli THoolia prin tis THiakopes moo.
I had a lot of work before my vacation.

To form the past tense, add the following endings to the future stem. The endings shown above for the past of έχω/*eho*, are typical of past tense endings for most other verbs. Remember that most verbs change their form in the future, e.g. **θα αγοράσω**/*tha agoraso*. It is the future stem which is used to form the past tense.

αγόρασα	*agoras*	*-a*	I bought
αγόρασες		*-es*	you bought
αγόρασε		*-e*	he/she/it bought
αγοράσαμε		*-ame*	we bought
αγοράσατε		*-ate*	you bought
αγόρασαν		*-an*	they bought

Note that the stress is shifted to the syllable before that stressed in the present tense: αγοράζω/*agorAzo* (present), αγόρασα/*agOrasa* (past).

In the past tense the third syllable before the end of the word is always stressed. There are some verbs that consist only of two syllables in the present, e. g., παίζω/*pezo*, I play. In these cases, the prefix -ε/-e is added to the front of the verb and it is stressed, e. g. παίζω/*pezo* (present) becomes έπεξα/*Epeksa*, I played.

Examples of the past tense from this unit:

Present		Past	
νοικιάζω	*nikiAzo*	νοίκιασα	*nIkiasa*
σταματάω	*stamatAO*	σταμάτησα	*stamAtisa*
πληρώνω	*plirOno*	πλήρωσα	*plIrosa*
ξεκινάω	*ksekinAO*	ξεκίνησα	*ksekInisa*
τηλεφωνώ	*tilefonO*	τηλεφώνησα	*tilefOnissa*
στέλνω	*stElno*	έστειλα	*Estila*

Some examples:

Πληρώσαμε 5.000 δραχμές στο εστιατόριο!   We paid 5,000 drachmas in the
plirosame 5,000 THrahmes sto estiatorio!   restaurant!

έστειλες κάρτες στο γραφείο σου;   Did you send cards to your office?
estiles kartes sto grafio soo?

Δεν τηλεφώνησαν στο σπίτι τους χθες.   They didn't phone home yesterday.
THen tilefonisan sto spiti toos hthes.

things to do

6.3 Using the verbs given in the past tense, translate the words in parentheses into Greek and match them with the column on the right:

1	**Η βενζίνη** (has run out)	**a**	σταμάτησε
2	(I've had) **μια βλάβη**	**b**	έκλεψαν
3	**Το αυτοκίνητο** (stopped) **ξαφνικά**	**c**	έκοψα
4	(He's lost) **το πορτοφόλι του**	**d**	έπαθα
5	(They stole) **το διαβατήριό μου**	**e**	έχασε
6	(I've cut) **το δαχτυλό μου**	**f**	τελείωσε

6.4 Match the sentences with the parts of the body shown:

1 Έκοψα το δάχτυλό μου.
2 Με πονάει το δόντι μου.
3 Έπαθα έγκαυμα.
4 Το πόδι μου είναι πρησμένο.
5 Έχω πονοκέφαλο.
6 Με πονάει το στομάχι μου.

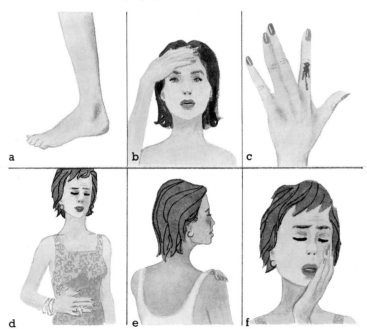

GREEK FESTIVALS

Being an Orthodox country, the Greek calendar is punctuated by many saint's days. As most people are named after saints – Giorgo(s) (George), Maria, etc. – they will celebrate their "name day" on the saint's day. This is in addition to their natural birthday. Cards and presents are exchanged on name days.

The central event in Greek traditional life is Easter. This is preceded by celebrations and festivities during Carnival, where people dress up and go out in boisterous groups (especially in the Plaka area); this festival is followed by Lent.

Easter begins with processions on Good Friday, and culminates in the midnight announcement "Christ is risen!" (Χριστός Ανέστη/*Hristos anesti!)* when people make a candlelight procession home from church. Traditionally lambs are roasted on a spit, and feasting ensues.

Cultural events Athens holds the Athens Festival of Music and Drama every summer, July to September. It centers on the Herod Atticus Theater (at the foot of the Acropolis), and offers a variety of classical and modern concerts, ballets, and drama. Performances start at 9 pm.

Epidavros–the ancient center of Greek drama, situated 150 km south of Athens in the Peloponnese – has a drama festival every summer. Excursions are plentiful from Athens, combining theater tickets with visits to ancient sites. Not to be missed.

For those with a thirst, don't miss a visit to the Wine Festival, which runs throughout the summer at Daphni, a few miles outside Athens. There's free wine to taste, and folk dancing to enjoy. Your hotel and the Greek Tourist Office will have details. Bus trips are organized there regularly.

Public holidays in Greece

January 1	New Year
January 6	Epiphany
1st day of Lent	"Clean Monday"
March 25	National Holiday – Independence Day
Easter Sunday, Monday	
May 1	Labor Day
August 15	Assumption
October 28	Όχι "No Day" – national holiday, when Greeks resisted the invasion of the Italians in 1941.

Days of the week

η Κυριακή	i kiriaki	Sunday	η Πέμπτη	i pempti	Thursday
η Δευτέρα	i THeftera	Monday	η Παρασκευή	i paraskevi	Friday
η Τρίτη	i triti	Tuesday	το Σάββατο	to savvato	Saturday
η Τετάρτη	i tetarti	Wednesday			

Seasons

η άνοιξη	i aniksi	spring	το φθινόπωρο	to fthinoporo	autumn
το καλοκαίρι	to kalokeri	summer	ο χειμώνας	o himonas	winter

Months of the year

There are two forms – both are masculine.

Ιανουάριος	ianooarios	γενάρης	yenaris	January
Φεβρουάριος	fevrooarios	Φλεβάρης	flevaris	February
Μάρτιος	martios	Μάρτης	martis	March
Απρίλιος	aprilios	Απρίλης	aprilis	April
Μάιος	maios	Μάης	mais	May
Ιούνιος	ioonios	Ιούνης	ioonis	June
Ιούλιος	ioolios	Ιούλης	ioolis	July
Αύγουστος	avgoostos			August
Σεπτέμβριος	septemvrios	Σεπτέμβρης	septemvris	September
Οκτώβριος	oktovrios	Οκτώβρης	oktovris	October
Νοέμβριος	noemvrios	Νοέμβρης	noemvris	November
Δεκέμβριος	THekemvrios	Δεκέμβρης	THekemvris	December

Πόσο του μηνός έχουμε;	posso too minos ehoome simera?	What's the date today?
είκοσι μία Μαρτίου	ikosi mia martioo	21st of March

SAYING GOODBYE

Μέχρι την επόμενη φορά/Until the next time

Peter is leaving soon, and has to tear himself away from Maria!

Maria: Τι κρίμα που φεύγεις σήμερα!
ti krima poo fevyis simera!

Peter: Και εγώ λυπάμαι. Πήγαμε σε τόσα ωραία μέρη. Φάγαμε όλα
ke ego lipame. Pigame se tossa orea meri. Fagame ola
τα ελληνικά φαγητά, και ήπιαμε τα καλύτερα κρασιά.
ta ellinika fayita, ke ipyame ta kalitera krasya.

Costas: Χαίρομαι που σου άρεσε τόσο πολύ η Ελλάδα.
herome poo soo arese tosso poli i ellатна.

Peter: Και οι Ελληνίδες (looking at Maria) μ'άρεσαν πολύ.
ke i elliniтнes m'aresan poli.

Maria: Μπορεί να σε δούμε στην Αγγλία φέτος.
bori na se тноumestin anglia fetos.

Peter: **Πότε θα έρθετε; Θα ήθελα να σας δείξω το Λονδίνο.**
pote tha erthete? tha ithela na sas тнikso to lonтнino.
Έχετε τη διεύθηνσή μου. Τηλεφωνείστε μου.
ehete tin тнiefthinsi moo. telefoniste moo.

Costas: (interrupting)Λοιπόν, Peter, **χάρηκα που σε γνώρισα.** Καλό
lipon, Peter, harika poo se gnorisa. kalo
ταξίδι και καλό χειμώνα.
taksiтнi, ke kalo himona.

Maria: Θα μου λείψεις Peter. Έλα ξανά γρήγορα.
tha moo lipsis, Peter. ela ksana grigora.

Peter: Αντίο σας, **μέχρι την επόμενη φορά.**
adio sas, mehri tin epomeni fora.

Useful words and phrases from the dialogue

Τι κρίμα!	*ti krima!*	What a pity!
λυπάμαι	*lipame*	I regret (it)/I'm sorry
πήγαμε	*pigame*	we went
Σε τόσα ωραία μέρη	*se tossa orea meri*	to so many nice places
φάγαμε	*fagame*	we ate
ήπιαμε	*ipyame*	we drank
τα καλύτερα κρασιά	*ta kalitera krasia*	the best wines
χαίρομαι	*herome*	I'm glad
σου άρεσε	*soo arese*	you liked
η Ελληνίδα,-ες	*i elliniΤΗa -es*	Greek woman/women
μπορεί	*bori*	maybe
φέτος	*fetos*	this year
Πότε θα έρθετε;	*pote tha erthete?*	When will you come?
να σας δείξω	*na sas ΤΗikso*	to show you
Χάρηκα που σε γνώρισα.	*harika poo se gnorisa.*	Glad to have met you.
Καλό ταξίδι.	*kalo taksiΤΗi.*	Bon voyage.
Καλό χειμώνα.	*kalo himona.*	Have a good winter.
Θα μου λείψεις.	*tha moo lipsis*	I'll miss you.
Έλα ξανά γρήγορα.	*ela ksana grigora.*	Come back quickly.
Αντίο.	*adio.*	Goodbye.
Μέχρι την επόμενη φορά	*mehri tin epomeni fora.*	Until the next time.

Other useful phrases

Ελπίζω να ξανάρθεις σύντομα.
elpizo na se/sas ksanaΤΗο sindoma.
I hope to see you again soon.

Λυπάμαι που δεν μπορείς/μπορείτε να μείνεις/μείνετε.
lipame poo ΤΗen boris/borite na minis/minete.
I'm sorry you can't stay.

Θα έρθεις του χρόνου, μου το υπόσχεσαι;
tha erthis too hronoo, moo to ipos-hese?
You'll come next year, do you promise me?

Πρέπει να φύγω/φύγουμε.
prepi na figo/figoome.
I/we have to leave.

Ασφαλώς θα έρθω ξανά
Of course I'll come again

Anne is at a bouzouki place with Yiannis and Eleni Vazakas and friends. It's her last evening in Athens.

Friend: **Να σας συστηθώ**, Σπύρος Νουσίου.
na sas sistitho. spiros Noosioo.

Anne: Anne Johnson. Χαίρω πολύ. **Είμαι η φίλη του κυρίου Βαζάκα.**
Anne Johnson. hero poli. ime i fili too kirioo vazaka.

Friend: Πρώτη φορά έρχεστε στην Ελλάδα;
proti fora erheste stin ellaтнa?

Anne: Ναι. Πέρασα μια θαυμάσια εβδομάδα στην Αθήνα.
ne. perasa mia thavmasia evтнomaтнa stin athina.

Friend: Πώς σας φάνηκε ο ελληνικός καιρός;
pos sas fanike o ellinikos keros?

Anne: Ήτανε θαυμάσιος! Βέβαια, έκανε πολύ ζέστη αλλά αυτό
Itane thavmasios! Vevea, ekane poli zesti alla afto
θέλουμε εμείς οι Άγγλοι.
theloome emis i angli.

Eleni: Πώς πέρασες στις διακοπές σου Ανν;
pos perases stis тнiakopes soo Anne?

Anne: **Χάρη σε σας είδα όλα τα αξιοθέατα της Αθήνας.** πάντα θα
hari se sas, iтнa ola ta aksiotheata tis athinas. panda tha
θυμάμαι το ταξίδι που κάναμε στους Δελφούς.
thimame to taksiтнi poo kaname stoos тнelfoos.

Yiannis: **Ας πιούμε στην υγεία της Anne. Να έρθεις ξανά του χρόνου.**
as pyoome stin iyia tis Anne. na erthis ksana too hronoo.

Anne: **Ασφαλώς θα έρθω ξανά. Ευχαριστώ για όλα.**
asfalos tha ertho ksana. efharisto ya ola.

Useful words and phrases from the dialogue

Να σας συστηθώ.	na sas sistitho.	Let me introduce myself.
ο φίλος/η φίλη	o filos, i fili	friend (masc./fem)
πέρασα	perasa	I've spent
πώς σας φάνηκε . . .;	pos sas fanike . . . ?	How did . . . seem to you?
χάρη σε σας	hari se sas	thanks to you
είδα	iTHa	I saw
τα αξιοθέατα	ta aksiotheata	the sights
πάντα θα θυμάμαι	panda tha thimame	I'll always remember
που κάναμε	poo kaname	that we made
Να έρθεις ξανά.	na erthis ksana.	Come again.
Ας πιούμε στην υγεία.	as pyoome stin iyia.	Let's drink to health.
του χρόνου	too hronoo	next year
Ασφαλώς θα έρθω ξανά.	Asfalos tha ertho ksana.	Of course I'll come again.

Socializing

Έχετε παιδιά;	ehete peTHia?	Do you have any children?
Έχω ένα γιό και μία κόρη.	eho ena yo ke mia kori.	I have a son and a daughter.
Πόσων χρονών είναι;	poson hronon ine?	How old is/are he/she/they?
Είστε παντρεμένος/η;	iste pandremenos/i?	Are you married?

Farewells

Ο κύριος και κυρία . . . ήτανε πολύ καλοί μαζί μου.
i kirios ke i kiria . . . itane poli kali mazi moo.
Mr. and Mrs. . . . have been very good to me.

Όταν έρθετε στην Αγγλία θα μείνετε στο σπίτι μου.
otan erthete stin anglia tha minete sto spiti moo.
When you come to England you'll stay at my house.

Μακάρι να έμενα ακόμα μια εβδομάδα.
makari na emena akoma mia evTHomaTHa.
I wish I could stay another week.

things to do

7.1 **a**   You are telling a Greek friend what you liked and didn't like during your vacation.

1   Greek food/liked
2   traffic in Athens/didn't like
3   Greek people/liked
4   stuffed vine leaves/didn't like

b   . . . and what you and your friends did.

5   We went to Sounion.
6   We saw the Acropolis.

7 We ate moussaka every day (!)
8 We drank retsina every night (!!)
9 We went on (lit. made) a trip to Epidavros.
10 We had a wonderful time!

7.2 You are at a party with some Greek people:

Greek: **Να σας συστηθώ. Με λένε Δημήτρη Τσεκούρα.**
You: (introduce yourself)
Greek: **Μιλάτε ελληνικά πολύ καλά. Από που είστε;**
You: (say where you're from)
Greek: **Σας αρέσει η Ελλάδα;**
You: (of course you do – say it's your second time)
Greek: **Σε ποιά νησιά πήγατε;**
You: (say you went to Aegina, Hydra, and Poros)
Greek: **Θα έρθετε ξανά του χρόνου;**
You: (say you'll come back, certainly)

KEY TO EXERCISES

1.1. 1 Καλημέρα σας.
2 Καλησπέρα σας. 3 Γειά σου.
4 Γειά σας/χαίρετε.
1.2 1 Θέλω ένα μονόκλινο.
2 Θέλω ένα δίκλινο. 3 Θέλω ένα δίκλινο με ντους. 4 Θέλω ένα μονόκλινο με μπάνιο. 5 Θέλω ένα τρίκλινο με μπάνιο.
1.3 1 **You:** Καλημέρα. **You:** Το όνομά μου είναι . . . **You:** Ορίστε το διαβατήριό μου. **You:** Τι ώρα έχει πρωινό;
1.4 1 τρία 2 δώδεκα 3 δεκαεπτά.
4 δέκα. 5 δεκατέσσερα.
1.5 1 Θέλω τσάι με γάλα, αυγά και μπέικον. 2 Θέλει καφέ, τοστ και μαρμελάδα. 3 Θέλουμε πορτοκαλάδα. 4 Θέλει τσάι με λεμόνι, τοστ, βραστό αυγό.

2.1 You: Από τη Αγγλία. **You:** Ειμαι . . . **You:** Ναι, με την γυναίκα μου Άντρα μου/με μερικούς φίλους. **You:** Τρεις μέρες. **You:** Στο Ξενοδοχείο "Ακρόπολη".
2.2 1 Τι ώρα φτάνει . . . **Answer** Φεύγει στις δέκα και μισή.
2 φεύγει . . . **Answer** Φεύγει στις έντεκα παρά τέταρτο. 3 Πόση ώρα κάνει . . . . **Answer** Κάνει μία ώρα και δεκαπέντε λεπτά. 4 Πόσα λεωφορεία πηγαίνουν; **Answer** Πέντε.
2.3 1 Η ώρα είναι τρεις το πρωί.
2 Η ώρα είναι οκτώ και μισή το πρωί. 3 Η ώρα είναι δώδεκα παρά πέντε το μεσημέρι. 4 Η ώρα είναι δώδεκα το μεσημέρι. 5 Η ώρα είναι δύο και μισή το απόγευμα. 6 Η ώρα είναι έξη και μισή το βράδυ.

3.1 1 ένα μέτριο. 2 ένα σκέτο, ένα γλυκό. 3 δύο μέτριους. 4 μία μπύρα. 5 δύο μπύρες. 6 τρείς κοκα-κόλες.
3.2 You: Το λογαριασμό, παρακαλώ. **You:** Συγνώμη, δύο μπύρες ένα τοστ. **You:** Πόσο κάνουν; **You:** Ορίστε τριακόσες δραχμές . . . Εντάξει.

3.3 You: μία καλαμαράκια, μία χταπόδι, μιά ταραμοσαλάτα. **You:** μισό κιλό μπαρμπούνια και δύο πατάτες τηγανητές **You:** ένα μπουκάλι ρετσίνα και μία σόδα. **You:** και μία χωριάτικη, παρακαλώ Total bill 4.380δρχ
3.4 1b. 2e. 3f. 4a. 5d. 6c.

4.1 1c. 2d. 3a. 4b.
4.2 1 ένα κιλό μήλα. 2 δύο κονσέρβες χυμό ντομάτας. 3 ένα πακέτο ζάχαρη. 4 ένα λίτρο νερό.
4.3 1 Δεν μ'αρέσει το χταπόδι.
2 Δεν μ' αρέσουν τα σταφύλια.
3 Μ' αρέσει το Ελληνικό τυρί.
4 Δεν μ' αρέσουν τα ελληνικά τσιγάρα.
4.4 You: Έχετε αυτά τα παπούτσια στο μέγεθός μου; **You:** Στην Αγγλία είμαι μέγεθος έξη. Τι μέγεθος είναι αυτό στήν Ελλάδα; **You:** Μου αρέσουν τα μπλε. **You:** Είναι λίγο μεγάλα. Μπορώ να δοκιμάσω το μέγεθος τριάντα οκτώ; **You:** εντάξει θα πάρω τα καφέ, μέγεθος τριάντα οχτώ.
4.5 1 Μπορώ να δω τον κατάλογο παρακαλώ; 2 Μπορούμε να έχουμε ένα τραπέζι για τέσσερις παρακαλώ; 3 Που μπορώ να βρώ φαρμακείο ; 4 Μπορώ να δοκιμάσω αυτό το φόρεμα παρακαλώ;

5.1 1 Τι ώρα φεύγει το πλοίο;
2 Πόσο κάνει το εισιτήριο; 3 Πόση ώρα κάνει το ταξίδι; 4 Τι ώρα γυρίζει το πλοίο; 5 Που θα φάμε μεσημεριανό; 6 Πρέπει ν'αγοράσω τα εισιτήρια τώρα;
5.2 You: Είναι ελεύθερη αυτή η θέση; **You:** Όχι, πρέπει να κατευώ στην Γλυφάδα. **You:** Όχι δεν είμαι σίγουρος/η. Μπορείτενα μου πείτε που να κατευώ; **You:** Ναι, αλλά φεύγω σε δύο μέρες.

5.3 1 υπάρχουν θέσεις για απόψε;
2 Πόσο κάνουν τα εισητήρια;
3 Θέλω τέσσερα εισητήρια.
4 Πόσο κάνουν όλα μαζί;
5 Τι ώρα αρχίζει η παράσταση; τι ώρα τελειώνει η παράσταση;
5.4 You: Τι παίζει στο σινεμά απόψε; **You:** Τι άλλο μπορούμε να κάνουμε; **You:** Πρέπει να κλείσουμε τραπέζι; **You:** Ναι, ένα τραπέζι για δύο στις εννέα και μισή.

6.1 You: Θέλω να νοικιάσω . . . με τέσσερις πόρτες. **You:** . . . ένα φτηνό αυτοκίνητο. **You:** Για τρεις μέρες.
6.2 1 Γεμίστε το με σούπερ.
2 Ελέγξτε το λάδι σας παρακαλώ.
3 Πάει αυτός ο δρόμος στην Αθήνα;
4 Πόσα χιλιόμετρα είναι μέχρι την Αθήνα;

6.3 1f. 2d. 3a. 4e. 5b. 6c.
6.4 1c. 2f. 3e. 4a. 5b. 6d.

7.1 1 Μ'αρέσει το ελληνικό φαγητό.
2 Δεν μ'άρεσει η κίνηση στην Αθήνα. 3 Μ'άρεσαν οι Έλληνες.
4 Δεν μ'αρέσαν οι ντολμάδες.
5 Πήγαμε στο Σούνιο. 6 Είδαμε την Ακρόπολη. 7 Φάγαμε μουσακά κάθε μέρα. 8 Ήπιαμε ρετσίνα κάθε βραδυ.
9 Κάναμε ένα ταξίδι στην Επίδαυρο.
10 Περάσαμε πολύ ωραία.
7.2 You: Με λένε . . . **You:** Είμαι από . . . **You:** Ασφαλώς-Είναι η δεύτερη φορά που έρχομαι. **You:** Πήγα στην Αίγινα, στην Ύδρα στον Πόρο. **You:** Ασφαλώς θα έρθω ξανά.

TOPIC VOCABULARY

ENGLISH–GREEK WORDLISTS

Professions/jobs

accountant	*logistis*/λογιστής **(f.)**
archeologist	*arheologos*/αρχαιολόγος **(m.)**
bank clerk	*ipallilos trapezis*/υπάλληλος τραπέζης **(m., f.)**
businessman/woman	*epihirimatias*/επιχειρηματίας **(m., f.)**
civil servant	*тHimosios ipallilos*/δημόσιος υπάλληλος **(m., f.)**
computer operator	*hirist-is/-ria kompiooter*/χειριστ-ής **(m.)** -ρια **(f.)** κομπιούτε
dentist	*отHondiatros*/οδοντίατρος **(m., f.)**
designer	*sheтHiastis/-ria*/σχεδιαστ-ής **(m.)** -ρια **(f.)**
director	*тHiefthind-is/-ria*/διευθηντ-ής **(m.)** ρια **(f.)**
doctor	*giatros*/γιατρός **(m., f.)**
electrician	*ilectrologos*/ηλεκτρολόγος **(m.)**
employee	*ipallilos*/υπάλληλος **(m., f.)**
engineer	*mihanikos*/μηχανικός **(m.)**
factory worker	*ergat-is/-ria ergostasiou*/εργάτ-ης **(m.)** --ρια **(f.)** εργοστασίο
farmer	*agrot-is/-ria*/αγρότης **(m.)** -ρια **(f.)**
hairdresser	*komoti-is/-ria*/κομμωτής **(m.)** -τρια **(f.)**
housewife	*nikokira*/νοικοκυρά **(f.)**
interpreter	*тHiermineas*/διερμηνέας **(m., f.)**
journalist	*тHimosiografos*/δημοσιογράφος **(m., f.)**
lawyer	*тHikigoros*/δικηγόρος **(m., f.)**
mechanic	*tehnitis*/τεχνίτης **(m.)**
nurse	*nosokoma*/νοσοκόμα **(f.)**
plumber	*iтHravlikos*/υδραυλικός **(m.)**
policeman	*astinomikos*/αστυνομικός **(m.)**
retired	*sintaksioohos*/συνταξιούχος **(m., f.)**
sales rep	*andiprosopos poliseon*/αντιπρόσωπος πολήσεων
secretary	*grammateas*/γραμματές **(m., f.)**
shop assistant	*ipallilos katastimatos*/υπάλληλος καταστήματος
social worker	*kinonik-os/-i litoorgos*/κοινωνικ-ός **(m.)**-ή **(f.)** λειτουργός
teacher	*тHaskal-os/-a*/δάσκαλος **(m.)**-α **(f.)**
technician	*tehnikos*/τεχνικός **(m.)**
unemployed	*anergos/-i*/άνεργος **(m.)** -η **(f.)**

Clothes

athletic shoes	*athlitika papootsia*/αθλητικά παπούτσια **(n.)**
bag	*tsanda*/τσάντα **(f.)**
belt	*zoni*/ζώνη **(f.)**
bikini	*bikini*/μπικίνι **(n.)**
blouse	*blooza*/μπλούζα **(f.)**
boots	*botes*/μπότες **(f.)**
bra	*soutien*/σουτιέν **(n.)**
briefs/underpants	*kilota*/κιλώτα **(f.)**
cardigan	*zaketa*/ζακέτα **(f.)**
coat	*palto*/παλτό **(n.)**
dress	*forema*/φόρεμα **(n.)**
gloves	*gandia*/γάντια **(n.)**
handkerchief	*mandili*/μαντίλι **(n.)**
hat	*kapello*/καπέλλο **(n.)**

jacket	*zaketa*/ζακέτα (**f.**)
jeans	*tzins*/τζηνς (**n.**)
nightdress	*nihtiko*/νυχτικό (**n.**)
pajamas	*pitzames*/πυντζάμες (**f.**)
raincoat	*aTHiavroho*/αδιάβροχο (**n.**)
sandals	*peTHila*/πέδιλα (**n.**)
scarf	*kaskol*/κασκώλ (**n.**)
shirt	*pookamiso*/πουκάμισο (**n.**)
shoes	*papootsia*/παπούτσια (**n.**)
skirt	*foosta*/φούστα (**f.**)
slippers	*pandofles*/παντόφλες (**f.**)
stockings	*kaltses*/κάλτσες (**f.**)
suit men	*kostoomi*/κουστόυμι (**n.**)
women	*tayier*/ταγιέρ (**n.**)
sweater	*blooza*/μπλούζα (**f.**)
sweatshirt	*fanella*/φανέλλα (**f.**)
swimsuit	*mayio*/μαγιώ (**n.**)
teeshirt	*mako blooza*/μακώ μπλούζα (**f.**)
tie	*gravata*/γραβάτα (**f.**)
tights	*kalson*/καλσόν (**n.**)
trousers	*pandeloni*/παντελόνι (**n.**)

Colors

color	*hroma*/χρώμα (**n.**)
beige	*bez*/μπέζ (**n.**)
black	*mavro*/μαύρο (**n.**)
blue	*ble*/μπλέ (**n.**)
brown	*kafe*/καφέ (**n.**)
green	*prasino*/πράσινο (**n.**)
gray	*gri*/γκρι (**n.**)
orange	*portokali*/πορτοκαλί (**n.**)
pink	*roz*/ροζ (**n.**)
red	*kokkino*/κόκκινο (**n.**)
white	*aspro*/άσπρο (**n.**)
yellow	*kitrino*/κίτρινο (**n.**)
dark/light	*skooro/anihto*/σκούρο ανοιχτό
purple	*mov, porfiro*/μώβ (**n.**) πορφυρό (**n.**)

Materials

acrylic	*akrilikos*/ακρυλικός/η/ο
cotton	*vamvakeros*/βαμβακερός/η/ο
denim	*tzin*/τζην
fur	*gooninos/i/o*/γούνινος/η/ο
leather	*THermatinos/i/o*/δερμάτινος/η/ο
nylon	*nailon*/νάιλον
silk	*metaksotos/i/o*/μεταξωτός/η/ο
suede	*kastorinos/i/o*/καστόρινος/η/ο
wool	*mallinos*/μάλλινος/η/ο

Pharmacy

antimosquito burner tablets	*Spira–Mat/Σπίρα -ματ* *Spira–mat tablettes/ταμπλέτες*
antiseptic	*antisiptikos/i/o/αντισηπτικός/η/ο*
aspirin	*aspirini/ασπιρίνη* **(f.)**
bandage	*epiτΗesmos/επίδεσμος* **(m.)**
capsule	*kapsoola/κάψουλα* **(f.)**
condom	*profilaktiko/προφυλακτικό* **(n.)**
contraceptive	*andisilliptiko/αντισυλληπτικό* **(n.)**
contraceptive pill	*andisilliptiko hapi/αντισυλλιπτικό χάπι* **(n.)**
cotton	*vamvaki/βαμβάκι* **(n.)**
cough drops	*pastillies yia to lemo/παστίλλιες για το λαιμό* **(f.)**
cough syrup	*siropi yia to viha/σιρόπι για το βήχα* **(n.)**
eyedrops	*stagones yia ta matia/σταγόνες για τα μάτια*
laxative	*kathartiko/καθαρτικό* (n.)
medicine	*farmako/φάρμακο* **(n.)**
painkiller	*pafsipono/παυσίπονο* **(n.)**
pill	*hapi/χάπι* **(n.)**
adhesive bandage	*tsiroto, emblastro/τσιρότο, έμπλαστρο* (n.)
prescription	*sindayi/συνταγή* **(f.)**
sanitary napkin	*servietes iyias/σερβιέτες υγείας* **(f.)**
tampon	*tampon/ταμπόν* **(n.)**
suntan lotion/oil	*andiliaki krema/laτΗi/αντηλιακή κρέμα/λάδι* **(n.)**
suppository	*ipotheto/υπόθετο* **(n.)**
thermometer	*thermometro/θερμόμετρο* **(n.)**

Toiletries

aftershave	*losion yia meta to ksirisma/λοσιόν για μετά το ξύρισμα*
baby food	*peτΗikes trofes/παιδικές τροφές* **(n.)**
brush	*voortsa/βούρτσα* (f.)
comb	*htena/χτένα* **(f.)**
contact lens	*fakos epafis/φακός επαφής* **(n.)**
cream	*krema/κρέμα* **(f.)**
deodorant	*aposmitiko/αποσμητικό* **(n.)**
disposable diapers	*panes mias hriseos/πάνες μιάς χρήσεως*
lipstick	*krayion/κραγιόν* **(n.)**
perfume	*aroma/άρωμα* **(n.)**
razor	*ksiristiki mihani/ξυριστική μηχανή* **(f.)**
razor blade	*ksirafi/ξυράφι* **(n.)**
safety pin	*paramana/παραμάνα* **(f.)**
shampoo	*sampooan/σαμπουάν* **(n.)**
shaving cream	*krema ksirismatos/κρέμα ξυρίσματος* **(n.)**
shaving foam	*afros ksirismatos/αφρός ξυρίσματος* **(m.)**
sunglasses	*yialia ilioo/γυαλιά ηλίου* **(n.)**
tissue	*hartomandila/χαρτομάντηλα* **(n.)**
toilet paper	*harti tooalettas/χαρτί τουαλέττας* **(f.)**
toothbrush	*oτΗondovoortsa/οδοντόβουρτσα* **(f.)**
toothpaste	*oτΗondopasta/οδοντόπαστα* **(f.)**

TOPIC VOCABULARY

Shops

Food and drink

baker	*foornos*/φούρνος **(m.)**
butcher	*kreopolio*/κρεοπολέιο **(n.)**
pastry	*zaharoplastio*/ζαχαροπλαστέιο **(n.)**
dairy	*galaktopolio*/γαλακτοπολείο **(n.)**
fish	*psaraτHiko*/ψαράδικο **(n.)**
produce market	*manaviko*/μανάβικο **(n.)**
grocer	*bakaliko*/μπακάλικο **(n.)**
market	*agora*/αγορά **(f.)**
supermarket	*soopermarket*/σούπερ μάρκετ **(n.)**
wine	*kava*/κάβα **(f.)**

other

bank	*trapeza*/τράπεζα **(f.)**
bookstore	*vivliopolio*/βιβλιοπολέιο **(n.)**
camping supplies	*iτΗi kataskinosis*/είδη κατασκήνωσης **(f.)**
pharmacy	*farmakio*/φαρμακείο **(n.)**
clothes women	*yinekia*/γυναικεία
men	*andrika*/αντρικά
department store	*katastima*/κατάστημα **(n.)**
dry cleaners	*katharistirio*/καθαρηστήριο **(n.)**
hairdressers	*kommotirio*/κομμωτήριο **(n.)**
laundry	*plindirio*/πλυντήριο **(n.)**
newsstand	*periptero*/περίπτερο **(n.)**
post office	*tahiτΗromio*/ταχυδρομείο **(n.)**
shoe store	*katastima papootsion*/κατάστημα παπουτσιών **(n.)**
stationers	*hartopolio*/χαρτοπολείο **(n.)**
tobacconist	*kapnopolio*/καπνοπολείο **(n.)**
toyshop	*katastima pehniτΗion*/κατάστημα παιχνιδιών **(n.)**

Parts of a car

accelerator	*gazi*/γκάζι **(n.)**
battery	*bataria*/μπαταρία **(f.)**
hood	*kapo*/καπώ **(n.)**
trunk	*port bagaz*/πορτ μπαγκάζ **(n.)**
brakes	*frena*/φρένα **(n.)**
bulb	*glombos*/γλόμπος **(m.)**
fender	*profilaktiras*/προφυλακτήρας **(m.)**
carburetor	*karbirater*/καρμπιρατέρ **(n.)**
clutch	*ambrayiaz*/αμπραγιάζ **(n.)**
generator	*yennitria*/γεννήτρια **(f.)**
engine	*mihani*/μηχανή **(f.)**
exhaust	*eksatmisi*/εξάτμηση **(f.)**
fanbelt	*imas*/ιμάς **(m.)**
fuse	*asfalia*/ασφάλεια **(f.)**
gas	*venzini*/βενζίνη **(f.)**
gas tank	*deposito venzinis*/ντεπόζιτο βενζίνης **(n.)**
gear	*tahitita*/ταχύτητα **(f.)**
gearbox	*kivotio tahititon*/κιβώτιο ταχυτήτων

headlight	*brostino fanari*/μπροστινό φανάρι (n.)
horn	*klakson*/κλάξον (n.)
jack	*grillos*/γρύλλος (n.)
license plate	*pinakiTHa*/πινακίδα (f.)
lights head	*brostina fota*/μπροστινά φώτα (n.)
rear	*piso fota*/πίσω φώτα (n.)
side	*plaina fota*/πλαϊνά φώτα (n.)
brake	*fota frenon*/φώτα φρένων (n.)
indicator	*flas*/φλας (n.)
seat	*thesi*/θέση (f.)
seatbelt	*zoni asfalias*/ζώνη ασφαλείας (f.)
spark plug	*boozi*/μπουζί (n.)
starter	*ekkinitir*/εκκινητήρ (m.)
steering wheel	*timoni*/τιμώνι (n.)
tire	*lastiho*/λάστιχο (n.)
wheel	*roTHa*/ρόδα (f.)
windshield	*parbriz*/μπαμπρίζ (n.)
windshield wiper	*ialokatharistires*/υαλοκαθαριστήρες (n.)

Food

Fruit

apple	*milo*/μήλο (n.)
banana	*banana*/μπανάνα (f.)
cherry	*kerasi*/κεράσι (n.)
fig	*siko*/σύκο (n.)
grape white	*stafili aspro*/σταφύλι άσπρο (n.)
black	*mavro*/μαύρο
lemon	*lemoni*/λεμόνι (n.)
melon	*peponi*/πεπόνι (n.)
nectarine	*nektarini*/νεκταρίνι (n.)
orange	*portokali*/πορτοκάλι (n.)
peach	*roTHakino*/ροδάκινο (n.)
pear	*ahlathi*/αχλάδι (n.)
pineapple	*ananas*/ανανάς (μ)
tangerine	*mandarini*/μανταρίνι (n.)
watermelon	*karpoozi*/καρπούζι (n.)

Vegetables

beans french	*fasolakia prasina*/φασολάκια πράσινα (n.)
broad	*kookia*/κουκιά (n.)
cabbage	*lahano*/λάχανο (n.)
carrot	*karoto*/καρότο (n.)
cucumber	*angoori*/αγγούρι (n.)
eggplant	*melitzana*/μελιντζάνα (f.)
garlic	*skorTHo*/σκόρδο (n.)
lettuce	*marooli*/μαρούλι (n.)
olives	*elies*/ελιές (f.)
onion	*kremmiTHi*/κρεμμύδι (n.)

TOPIC VOCABULARY

pea	*bizeli*/μπιζέλι (n.)
pepper	*piperia*/πιπεριά (f.)
potato	*patata*/πατάτα (f.)
salad (peasant) salad	*salata horiatiki*/σαλάτα χωριάτικη (f.)
shrimp salad	*gariтноsalata*/γαριδοσαλάτα (f.)
green salad	*prasini salata*/πράσινη σαλάτα (f.)
russian salad	*rossiki salata*/ρώσικη σαλάτα (f.)
tomato	*domata*/ντομάτα (f.)
vine leaves (stuffed)	*dolmaтнes*/ντολμάδες (m.)
yoghurt and garlic dip	*tzatziki*/τζατζίκι (n.)

Fish

cod	*bakaliaros*/μπακαλιάρος (m.)
crab	*kavoori*/καβούρι (n.)
crayfish	*karaviтнa*/καραβίδα (f.)
lobster	*astakos*/αστακός (m.)
mussels	*miтнia*/μίδια (n.)
octopus	*htapoтнi*/χταπόδι (n.)
red mullet	*barbooni*/μπαρμπούνι (n.)
sardine	*sarтнella*/σαρδέλλα (f.)
shrimps	*gariтнes*/γαρίδες (f.)
squid	*kalamari*/καλαμάρι (n.)
(baby) squid	*kalamaraki*/καλαμαράκι (n.)
swordfish	*ksifias*/ξιφίας (m.)
tuna	*tonos*/τόνος (m.)

Meat

bacon	*beikon*/μπέικον (n.)
beef	*voтнino*/βοδινό (n.)
chicken	*kotopoolo*/κοτόπουλο (n.)
chops	*brizoles*/μπριζόλες (f.)
ham	*zambon*/ζαμπόν (n.)
kebab	*soovlaki*/σουβλάκι (n.)
lamb	*arni*/αρνί (n.)
lamb chops	*paiтнakia*/παϊδάκια (n.)
meatballs	*kefteтнes*/κεφτέδες (m.)
pork	*hirino*/χοιρινό (n.)
sausage	*lookaniko*/λουκάνικο (n.)
steak	*brizola*/μπριζόλα (f.)
veal	*mos~hari*/μοσχάρι (n.)

Groceries

bread	*psomi*/ψωμί (n.)
biscuits	*biskota*/μπισκότα (n.)
butter	*vootiro*/βούτυρο (n.)
cake	*keik*/κέικ (n.)
cheese feta	*tiri feta*/τυρί φέτα (f.)
gouda	*tiri gooda*/τυρί γκούντα (n.)
cheese pie	*tiropitta*/τυρόπηττα (f.)

TOPIC VOCABULARY

coffee	*kafes*/καφές (m.)
cookies	*biskota*/μπισκότα (n.)
eggs	*avga*/αυγά (n.)
milk	*gala*/γάλα (n.)
nuts (pistachio)	*fistikia*/φυστίκια (n.)
oil	*laTHi*/λάδι (n.)
olive oil	*eleolaTHo*/ελαιόλαδο (n.)
pasta	*zimarika*/ζυμαρικά (n.)
pepper	*piperi*/πιπέρι (n.)
rice	*rizi*/ρύζι (n.)
salt	*alati*/αλάτι (n.)
spaghetti	*makaronia*/μακαρόνια (n.)
sugar	*zahari*/ζάχαρη (f.)
tea	*tsai*/τσάι (n.)
vinegar	*ksiTHi*/ξύδι (n.)
wine	*krasi*/κρασί (n.)
yoghurt	*yiaoorti*/γιαούρτι (n.)

Parts of the body

ankle	*astragalos*/αστράγαλος (m.)
arm	*bratso*/μπράτσο (n.)
back	*plati*/πλάτη (f.)
blood	*ema*/αίμα (n.)
bone	*kokkalo*/κόκκαλο (n.)
breast	*stithos*/στήθος (n.)
chest	*stithos*/στήθος (n.)
ear	*afti*/αφτί (n.)
elbow	*angonas*/αγκώνας (m.)
eye	*mati*/μάτι (n.)
face	*prosopo*/πρόσωπο (n.)
finger	*THahtilo*/δάχτυλο (n.)
foot	*pothi*/πόδι (n.)
hair	*mallia*/μάτια (n.)
hand	*heri*/χέρι (n.)
head	*kefali*/κεφάλι (n.)
heart	*kardia*/καρδιά (f.)
hip	*gofos*/γοφός (m.)
knee	*gonato*/γόνατο (n.)
leg	*piTHi*/πόδι (n.)
lips	*hilia*/χίλια (n.)
lungs	*pnevmones*/πνεύμονες (m.)
mouth	*stoma*/στόμα (n.)
muscle	*mis*/μυς (m.)
neck	*lemos*/λαιμός (m.)
nose	*miti*/μάτι (n.)
rib	*plevro*/πλευρό (n.)
shoulder	*omos*/ώμος (m.)
skin	*THerma*/δέρμα (n.)
stomach	*stomahi*/στομάχι (n.)
thigh	*miros*/μηρός (m.)
throat	*lemos*/λαιμός (m.)
thumb	*andihiras*/αντίχειρας (m.)

tooth	тнondi/δόντι (n.)
toe	тнahtilo/δάχτυλο (n.)
tongue	glossa/γλώσσα (f.)
waist	messi/μέση (f.)
wrist	karpos/καρπός (m.)

Sports and games

ball	balla/μπάλα (f.)
basketball	basket/μπάσκετ (n.)
beach	paralia/παραλία (f.)
boat	varka/βάρκα (f.)
canoe	kano/κανώ (n.)
canoeing	kano kano/κάνω κανώ
cards	trapooloharta/τραπουλόχαρτα (n.)
cycling	poτнilaτoτнromia/ποδηλατοδρομεία (f.)
dancing	horos/χορός (m.)
dinghy	mikri varka/μικρή βάρκα (f.)
fishing	psarema/ψάρεμα (n.)
floats (for kids' arms)	bratsakia/μπρατσάκια (n.)
golf	golf/γκόλφ (n.)
jogging	tsogging/τζόγκινγ (n.)
pedal boat	poτнilato thalassas/ποδήλατο θάλασσας (f.)
sailing	istioploia/ιστιοπλοία (f.)
skiing	ski/σκι (n.)
soccer	poτнosfero/ποδόσφαιρο (n.)
speedboat	kris-kraft/κρις-κράφτ (n.)
sunbathing	iliotherapia/ηλιοθεραπεία (f.)
swimming	kolimbi/κολύμπι (n.)
swimming pool	pisina/πισίνα (f.)
tennis	tennis/τέννις (n.)
tennis court	yepeτнo tennis/γήπεδο τέννις (n.)
tennis racket	raketa tennis/ρακέττα τέννις (f.)
volleyball	vollei bol/βόλλευ-μπώλ (n.)
walking	perpatima/περπάτημα (n.)
waterskiing	thalassio ski/θαλάσσιο σκι (n.)
windsurfing	gooindserfing/γουιντσέρφινγ (n.)

Leisure, entertainment, sightseeing

art gallery	galleri/γκαλερί (f.)
bar	bar/μπάρ (n.)
bouzouki place	kendro/κέντρο (n.)
castle	kastro/κάστρο (n.)
cathedral	katheτнrikos naos/καθεδρικός ναός (m.)
cave	spilia/σπηλιά (f.)
church	ekklisia/εκκλησία (f.)
cinema	kinimatografos/κινηματογράφος (m.)
coast	akti/ακτή (f.)
disco	diskotek/ντισκοτέκ (f.)
excursion	ekτнromi/εκδρομή (f.)
film	tenia/ταινία (f.)

island	*nisi*/νησί (n.)
lake	*limni*/λίμνη (f.)
monastery	*monastiri*/μοναστήρι (n.)
monument	*mnimio*/μνημείο (n.)
mountain	*voono*/βουνό (n.)
museum	*moosio*/μουσείο (n.)
nightclub	*nihterino kendro*/νυχτερινό κέντρο (n.)
restaurant	*estiatorio*/εστιατόριο (n.)
ruin	*eripio*/ερίπιο (n.)
sea	*thalassa*/θάλασσα (f.)
taverna	*taverna*/ταβέρνα (f.)
view	*thea*/θέα (f.)
wall	*tihos*/τοίχος (m.)

Weather

clear	*ethrios*/αίθριος
cloud	*sinnifo*/σύννεφο (n.)
cloudy	*sinnefiasmenos*/συννεφιασμένος
cold	*krio*/κρύο (n.)
cool	*THrosia*/δροσιά (f.)
drizzle	*psihalisma*/ψιχάλισμα (n.)
hot	*zestos*/ζεστός
lightning	*astrapi*/αστραπή (f.)
rain	*vrohi*/βροχή (f.)
rainy	*vroheros*/βροχερός
shower	*boorini*/μπουρίνι (n.)
sky	*ooranos*/ουρανός (m.)
sun	*ilios*/ήλιος (m.)
sunny	*liakaTHa*/λιακάδα (f.)
thunder	*vrondi*/βροντή (f.)
umbrella	*ombrella*/ομπρέλλα (f.)
wind	*anemos*/άνεμος (m.)
windy	*anemoTHis*/ανεμώδης

Souvenirs

classical copy (of an ancient design/statue)	*andigrafo*/αντίγραφο (n.)
handbag	*tsanda*/τσάντα (f.)
hand-made	*hiropiitos/i*/χειροποίητος, η, ο
head (statue)	*kefali (aglamatos)*/κεφάλι (αγάλματος)
jewelry	*kosmimata*/κοσμήματα (n.)
leather	*THerma*/δέρμα (n.)
leather goods	*THermatina iTHi*/δερμάτινα είδη (n.)
necklace	*kollie*/κολλιέ (n.)
pottery	*keramiki*/κεραμική (f.)
statue	*agalma*/άγαλμα (n.)
vase	*vazo*/βάζω (n.)
weave	*ifando*/υφαντό (n.)
worry beads	*komboloi*/κομπολόι (n.)

VOCABULARY

GREEK-ENGLISH VOCABULARY

Άγαλμα *agalma* (n.) statue
αγαπάω *agapao* to love
Αγγλία *Anglia* (f.) England
Αγγλίδα *Anglida* (f.) English(woman)
αγγλικά *anglika* (n.) English
    (language)
αγγλικός *anglikos* (m.) English
    (adjective)
Άγγλος *Anglos* (m.) English(man)
αγγούρι *angoori* (n.) cucumber
άγιος, αγία *ayios* (m.) ayia (f.) saint
αγοράζω *agorazo* to buy
άδεια οδηγήσεως *athia othigiseos* (f.)
    driver's license
αδελφή *athelfi* (f.) sister
αέρας *aeras* (m.) wind
ΑΔΙΕΞΟΔΟΣ *athieksothos* No through
    road
αεροδρόμιο, αερολιμένας *aerothromio,
    aerolimenas* (n.), (m.) airport
αεροπλάνο *aeroplano* (n.) airplane
αεροπορικώς *aeroporikos* by air
αίθουσα αναμονής *ethoosa anamonis*
    waiting room
αισθάνομαι *esthanome* to feel
ακτοφύλακας *aktofilakas* (m.) lifeguard
ακτή *akti* (f.) coast
ακριβό *akrivo* expensive
αλάτι *alati* (n.) salt
(να) αλλάξει,(αλλάζω) *(na)
    allaksi,(allazo)* to change
    (I change)
αλλεργικός *allergikos* allergic
αλλεργικό συνάχι *allergiko sinahi* (n.)
    hay fever
αλήθεια *alithia* really, actually
αλοιφή *alifi* (f.) ointment
αμέσως *amesos* immediately
άμμος *ammos* (f.) sand
αμφιθέατρο *amfitheatro* (n.)
    amphitheater
αμφορέας *amforeas* (m.) amphora
αναπτήρας *anaptiras* (m.) lighter
ΑΝΑΧΩΡΗΣΕΙΣ *anahorisis* departures
αναψυκτικά *anapsiktika* (n.)
    refreshments
ΑΝΔΡΩΝ *anthron* men (toilet)

άνθρωπος *anthropos* (m.) man
αντηλιακό (λαδι) *andilliako* (laτhi) (n.)
    suntan oil
αντισυλληπτικά χάπια *andisilliptika
    hapia* (n.) contraceptive (pills)
αντίο *andio* goodbye
άντρας *andras* (m.) man
απόιδειξη *apothiksi* (f.) receipt
ΑΝΟΙΚΤΟ *anikto* open
ΑΠΑΓΟΡΕΥΕΤΑΙ *apagorevete* it is
    forbidden
απέναντι *apenandi* opposite
απλώς *aplos* simply, just
απόγευμα *apoyevma* (n.) afternoon
αποσκευές *aposkeves* (f.) luggage
αρέσει(μ'αρέσει) *aressi* (m'aressi)
    I like (it)
μ' αρέσουν *m'aressoon* I like (them)
αριθμός *arithmos* (m.) number
αριστερά *aristera* left
αρνάκι *arnaki* (n.) lamp
αρνί *arni* (n.) mutton
άρρωστος *arrostos* ill, sick
αρχαιολογικός τόπος *arheologikos topos*
    (m.) archeological site
αρχαία *arhea* antiquities
αρχαία ελληνική τραγωδία *arhea
    elliniki tragoτhia* classical Greek
    tragedy
ασανσέρ *asanser* (n.) elevator
ασθενοφόρο *asthenoforo* (n.)
    ambulance
άσπρο *aspro* white
ασπιρίνη *aspirini* (f.) aspirin
αστράγαλος *astragalos* (m.) ankle
αστυνομία *astinomia* (f.) police
αστυνομικό τμήμα *astinomiko tmima*
    (n.) police station
ασφάλεια *asfalia* (f.) insurance
άσχημος καιρός *ashimos keros* (m.)
    bad weather
άτομα *atoma* (n.) people
αυγό *avgo* (n.) egg
αύριο *avrio* tomorrow
αυτοκίνητο *aftokinito* (n.) car
ΑΦΙΞΕΙΣ *Afiksis* Arrivals
Αχθοφόρε! *Ahthofore!* (m.) Porter!
αχλάδια *ahlathia* (n.) pears

VOCABULARY

Βαλίτσα *valitsa* (f.) suitcase
βάζο *vazo* (n.) vase
βάλτε(βάζω) *valte (vazo)* to put (I put)
βαμβακερό *vamvakero* cotton
βάρκα *varka* (f.) boat
βάρκα με μηχανή *varka me mihani* motorboat
βάρκα με πανί *varka me pani* sailboat
βέβαια, βεβαίως *vevea/veveos* of course
βαθειά *vathia* deep
βαπόρι *vapori* (n.) ship
βενζίνη (απλή) *venzini (apli)* (f.) gasoline (regular)
βερύκοκα *verikoka* (n.) apricots
βεράντα *veranda* (f.) verandah
βήχας *vihas* (m.) cough
βλάβη *vlavi* (f.) breakdown
βλέπω *vlepo* I see
βοήθεια! *voithia!* Help!
(να σας) βοηθήσει (βοηθάω) (na sas) *voithisi (voithao)* to help you (I help)
βουνό *voono* (n.) mountain
βούτυρο *vootiro* (n.) butter
βράδι *vraтні* (n.) evening
βραδινό *vraтнino* (n.) supper
βραστό *vrasto* boiled
βρέχει *vrehi* it is raining
βροχή *vrohi* (f.) rain

Γάλα *gala* (n.) milk
γαρίδα *gariтна* (f.) shrimp
γεμάτοι *yemati* full
γεμίστε(γεμίζω) *yemiste (yemizo)* fill (I fill)
γεύμα *yevma* (n.) meal
Γειά σου *yia soo* hello/goodbye (informal)
γερανός *yeranos* (n.) crane
γιαούρτι *yiaoorti* (n.) yoghurt
για *yia* for
για μια νύχτα *yia mia nihta* for one night
γιατρός *yiatros* (m.) doctor
γκαράζ *garaz* (n.) garage
γίνομαι *yinome* to become
γκαρσόν *garson* (n.) waiter
γκισέ *gisé* (n.) cash desk
γκρί *gri* gray
γλυκά *glika* (n.) desserts
γράμμα *gramma* (n.) letter

γραμματόσημα *grammatosima* (n.) stamps
γραμματοκιβώτιο *grammatokivotio* (n. mailbox
Γραφείο Τουρισμού *Grafio Toorismoo* (n.) Tourist Office
γρήγορα *grigora* quickly
γυαλιά ηλίου *yialia ilioo* (n.) sunglasses
γυναίκα *yineka* (f.) woman
ΓΥΝΑΙΚΩΝ *Yinekon* ladies (toilet)
γύρος *yiros* (m.) tour
γωνία *gonia* (f.) corner

Δείπνο *тніpno* (n.) dinner
δέκα *тнeka* ten
δεξιά *тнeksia* on the right
δεσποινίς *тнespinis* (f.) miss
Δευτέρα *тнeftera* (f.) Monday
διερμηνέας *тнiermineas* (m.) interpreter
διαβατήριο *тнiavatirio* (n.) passport
(να μου) δείξετε (δείχνω) (na moo) *тніksete (тніhno)* to show me (I show)
δελτίο καιρού *тнeltio keroo* (n.) weather forecast
διάλειμμα *тнialimma* (n.) intermissio
διαμέρισμα *тнiamerisma* (n.) flat
Διανυχτερεύον *тнianikterevon* open a night
διακόσια *тнiakosia* two hundred
διακοπές *тнiakopes* (f.) vacation
διάρροια *тнiaria* (f.) diarrhea
διασκεδάζω *тнiaskeтнazo* to enjoy myself
διασταύρωση *тнiastavrosi* (f.) crossroads
διεύθυνση *тнiefthinsi* (f.) address
δίκλινο *тніklino* (n.) double room
(Μας δίνετε) δίνω (Mas) *тнinete (тнino)* Would you give us (I give
δικηγόρος *тніkigoros* (m.) lawyer
δίκιο *тніkio* (n.) right
διόδια *тнioтнia* (n.) toll
διψάω *тніpsao* to be thirsty
δοκιμαστήρια *тнokimastiria* (n.) changing rooms
δοκιμάστε (τα) (δοκιμάζω) *тнokimaste (ta) (тнokimazo)* try (them) on, (I try on)
δολλάρια *тнollaria* (n.) dollars

VOCABULARY

δράμα *THrama* (n.) drama
δραχμή *THrahmi* (f.) drachma
δουλειά *THoolia* (f.) job
ΔΡΟΜΟΛΟΓΙΑ *THromologia* (n.) time tables
δρόμος *THromos* (m.) road street
δύο *THio* two
δροσιά *THrosia* (f.) cool (weather)
δύσκολα *THiskola* difficult
δυστύχημα *THistihima* (n.) accident
δυστυχώς *THistihos* unfortunately
δώδεκα *THOTHeka* twelve
δωμάτιο *THomatio* (n.) room
δώστε(μου), (δίνω) *THoste* (moo), (thino) give (me), (I give)

Εβδομάδα *evTHomaTHa* (f.) week
εβδομαδιαίος,α,ο *evTHomaTHieos* weekly
έγκαυμα *engavma* (n.) burn
έγκυος *engyos* (f.) pregnant
εγώ *ego* I
έγχρωμο φιλμ *enhromo film* (n.) color film
εδώ *eTHO* here
εθνική οδός *ethniki oTHos* (f.) main street
είκοσι *ikosi* twenty
είμαι *ime* I am
είμαστε *imaste* we are
εισητήριο *isitirio* (n.) ticket
εισητήριο με επιστροφή *isitirio me epistrofi* (n.) round-trip ticket
είσοδος *isoTHos* (f.) entrance
εκατό *ekato* a hundred
εκδρομή *ekTHromi* (f.) excursion
εκεί *eki* there
έκθεση *ekthesi* (f.) exhibition
εκεί πέρα *eki pera* over there
εκκλησία *ekklisia* (f.) church
εκείνος, η, ο *ekinos* that
εκπτώσεις *ekptosis* (f.) sales
έκοψα (κόβω) *ekopsa,* (kovo) I've cut (I cut)
έκαψα (καίω) *ekapsa* (keo) I´ve burned (I burn)
έκλεψαν (κλέβω) *eklepsan* (klevo) They stole (I steal)
ελάτε (έρχομαι) *elate* (erhome) come (I come)
Έλεγχος διαβατηρίων *elenhos THiavatirion* (m.) Passport Control
ελιές *elies* (f.) olives
Ελλάδα *Ellatha* (f.) Greece

Έλληνας *Ellinas* (m.) Greek (man)
Ελληνίδα *ElliniTHa* (f.) Greek (woman)
Ελληνικός, η, ο *Ellinikos* (n.) Greek (adjective)
Ελληνικά *Ellinika* (n.) Greek (language)
ένα *ena* one
ένας, μία ένα *enas, mia, ena* a, an
ένδεκα *enTHeka* eleven
ενενήντα *eneninda* ninety
εννιά *ennia* nine
εννιακόσια *enniakosia* nine hundred
ενοικιάσεις αυτοκινήτων *enikiasis aftokiniton* car rental
εντάξει *entaksi* it's all right
εξακόσια *eksakosia* six hundred
εξήντα *Eksinda* sixty
έξι *eksi* six
έξοδος *eksoTHos* (f.) exit
ΕΞΟΔΟΣ ΚΙΝΔΥΝΟΥ *EksoTHos kinTHinoo* emergency exit
εξώστης *Eksostis* (m.) upper circle
επιταγή *epitayi* (f.) order check
επιπλέον *epipleon* moreover
επιδόρπιο *epithorpio* (n.) dessert
επίδεσμος *epithesmos* (m.) bandage
να επιδιορθώσετε (επιδιορθώνω) *na epiTHiorthosete* (epiTHiorthono) to repair (I repair)
έπεσα, (πέφτω) *epesa (pefto)* I´ve fallen (I fall)
επικίνδυνος, η, ο *epikinTHinos,i, o* dangerous
επόμενος, η, ο *epomenos i,o* next
έπαθα (παθαίνω) *epatha(patheno)* I´ve suffered (I suffer)
επείγον *epigon* urgent
έπιασε φωτιά *epiase fotia* it's caught fire
επίσκεψη *episkepsi* (f.) visit
να έρθει (έρχομαι) *na erthi (erhome)* to come (I come)
(σας) ερχεται καλά *(sas) erhete kala* it fits you well
έσκασε το λάστιχο *eskase to lastiho* I've had a puncture
ερείπια *eripia* (n.) ruins
εσείς *esis* you (formal)
εσπρέσσο *espresso* (m.) espresso
εστιατόριο *estiatorio* (n.) restaurant
έτοιμο *etimo* ready
ευθεία *efthia* (f.) straight ahead
ευχαριστώ *efharisto* thank you

VOCABULARY

εφτά *efta* seven
εφτακόσια *eftakosia* seven hundred
έχετε καθόλου *ehete katholoo* . . .
  have you got any . . .
έχω κλείσει *eho klisi* I've reserved
έχασα (χάνω) *ehasa hano* I've lost
  (I lose)
εσύ *esi* you (informal)
εφημερίδα *efimeriTHa* (f.) newspaper
εύκολος, η, ο *efkolos, i, o* easy
Ζακέτα *zakéta* (f.) jacket
ζάχαρη *zahari* (f.) sugar
Ζαχαροπλαστείο *Zaharoplastio* (n.)
  pastry shop
ζέστη *zesti* (f.) heat
ζεστός, η, ο *zestos, i, o* hot
ζευγάρι *zevgari* (n.) pair
ζώνη *zoni* (f.) belt

Ήλιος *ilios* (m.) sun
ηλίαση *iliasi* (f.) sunstroke
ημερήσιος *imerisios a, o* daily
ημερομηνία *imerominia* (f.) date
ήρεμος, η, ο *iremos, i, o* calm (the sea)
ήμουνα (είμαι) *imoona (ime)* I was
  (I am)
ήσυχος, η, ο *isihos, i, o* quiet
ήπιαμε (πίνω) *ipiame (pino)* we drank
  (I drink)

Θάλασσα *thalassa* (f.) sea
θαλασσινά *thalassina* (n.) seafood
θαλάσσιο σκι *thalassio ski* (n.)
  waterski
θαυμάσιος, α, ο *thavmasios, a, o,*
  wonderful
θέα *thea* (f.) view
θέατρο *theatro* (n.) theater
θέλω . . . *thelo* I want/I'd like
θέλετε *thelete* Do you want/would
  you like
θερμοκρασία *thermokrasia* (f.)
  temperature
θέση *thesi* (f.) seat
θυμάμαι *thimame* I remember

καθαρός, η, ο *katharos,* clean, clear
καθένας *kathenas* everyone
κάθε *kathe* each
καθίστε (κάθομαι) *kathiste (kathomai)*
  sit (I sit)
καθρέφτης *kathreftis* (m.) mirror
καθυστέριση *kathisterisi* (f.) delay

(πόσο) καιρό . . . (*Poso) kero* . . . ?
  How long . . . ?
καιρός *keros* (m.) weather
καλά *kala* well
καλαμαράκια *kalamarakia* (n.) squid
καλημέρα *kalimera* good morning
καληνύχτα *kalinihta* good night
καλησπέρα *kalispera* good evening
καλός καιρός *kalos keros* good
  weather
καλσόν *kalson* (n.) tights
κάλτσες *kaltses* socks (f.) stockings
κάμπινγκ *kamping* (n.) campsite
κάνει ζέστη *kani zesti* it's hot
κανώ *kano* (n.) canoe
καλώς ωρίσατε *kalos orisate* welcom
καπέλλο *kapello* (n.) hat
καπνίζω *kapnizo* to smoke
καπουτσίνο *kapootsino* (m.)
  cappuccino
καράβι *karavi* (n.) boat
καραμέλλες *karamelles* (f.) candy
καρδιακός, η, ο *karTHiakos, i, o* pers
  suffering from his heart
καρέκλα *karekla* (f.) chair
καρότα *karota* (n.) carrots
καρπούζι *karpoozi* (n.) watermelon
κάρτα *karta* (f.) card
καρχαρίας *karharias* (m.) shark
κασσετόφωνο *kassetofono* (n.) tape
  recorder
καταλαβαίνω *katalaveno* to
  understand
κατάλογος *katalogos* (m.) menu
κατάστημα *katastima* (n.) store
κατάστρωμα *katastroma* (n.) deck
καφέ *kafe* brown
καφενείο *kafenio* (n.) café
καφές *kafes* (m.) coffee
κέικ *keik* (n.) cake
κέντρο *kendro* (n.) town
  center/bouzouki place
κεράσια *kerasia* (n.) cherries
κι εσείς *ki esis* and you (formal)
κι εσύ *ki esi* and you (informal)
κιθάρα *kithara* (f.) guitar
κιλό *kilo* (n.) kilo
κίνδυνος *kinTHinos* (m.) danger
κινηματογράφος *kinimatografos* (m.)
  cinema
κίτρινο *kitrino* yellow

VOCABULARY

κλειδί *kliTHi* (n.) key
κλειστός, η, ο *klistos, i, o* closed
κλείνω εισητήρια *klino isitiria* to reserve tickets
κοιτάω *kitao* to look at
κλοπή *klopi* (f.) theft
κόκα-κόλα *koka-kola* (f.) Coke
κόκκινο *kokkino* red
κολοκυθάκια *kolokithakia* zucchini
κόλπος *kolpos* (m.) gulf
κολύμπι *kolimbi* (n.) swimming
κολυμπώ *kolimbo* to swim
κολώνα *kolona* (f.) column
κονιάκ *koniak* (n.) brandy
κονσέρβα *konserva* (f.) can
κομμάτι *kommati* (n.) piece (of)
κοντός,η,ο *kondos, i, o* short
κοστίζει *kostizi* it costs
κοτόπουλο *kotopoolo* (n.) chicken
κουτάλι *kootali* (n.) spoon
κρασί άσπρο *krasi aspro* (n.) white wine
κρασι γλυκό *krasi gliko* (n.) sweet wine
κρασί κόκκινο *krasi kokkino* (n.) red wine
κρασί ξηρό *krasi ksiro* (n.) dry wine
κρέας *kreas* (n.) meat
κρεβάτι *krevati* (n.) bed
κρέμα ηλίου *krema ilioo* (n.) suntan cream
κρεοπωλείο *kreopolio* (n.) butcher's shop
κρύο *krio* cold
κτίριο *ktirio* (n.) building
κυματώδης *kimatoTHis* very rough (sea)
κυκλοφορία *kikloforia* (f.) traffic
κυρία *kiria* (f.) Mrs.
Κυριακή *kiriaki* (f.) Sunday
κύριος *kirios* (m.) Mr.
κωμωδία *komoTHia* (f.) comedy

Λάδι *laTHi* (n.) oil
λάδι ηλίου *laTHi ilioo* (n.) suntan oil
λαικός χορός *laikos horos* (m.) folk dancing
λάθος *lathos* (n.) mistake
λαχανικά *lahanika* (n.) vegetables
λεμονάδα *lemonaTHa* (f.) lemonade
λεμόνι *lemoni* (n.) lemon
λέξη *leksi* (f.) word
λεπτό *lepto* (n.) minute

λεφτά *lefta* (n.) money
λεωφορείο *leoforio* (n.) bus
λεωφόρος *leoforos* (f.) avenue
λιακάδα *liakaTHa* (f.) sunshine
λίρα *lira* (f.) English pound
λίγο *ligo* a little
λικέρ *liker* (n.) liqueur
λιμάνι *limani* harbor
λίτρο *litro* (n.) liter
λογαριασμός *logariasmos* (m.) bill
λουκάνικα *lookanika* (n.) sausages
λουτρά *lootra* (n.) baths
λύκος *likos* (m.) wolf
λυπάμαι *lipame* I'm sorry

Μαγιό *mayio* (n.) bathing suit
μαζί μας *mazi mas* with us
(να) μάθω (μαθαίνω) *na matho (matheno)* to learn (I learn)
μακριά *makria* far
μακώ (μπλούζα) *mako (blooza)* (f.) tee-shirt
μάλιστα *malista* yes, of course
μαρμελάδα *marmelaTHa* (f.) marmalade
μαρούλι *marooli* (n.) lettuce
μαύρο *mavro* black
μαχαίρι *maheri* (n.) knife
Μαντείο *mandio* (n.) Oracle
μέγεθος *meyethos* (n.) size
μεζέδες *mezeTHes* (m.) appetizers
μελιτζάνα *melitzana* (f.) eggplant
μενού *menoo* (n.) menu
μένω *meno* to live, to stay
μέρος *meros* (n.) part
μέχρι *mehri* till, to
με συγχωρείτε *me sinhorite* . . . Excuse me . . .
μέρα *mera* (f.) day
μεσημέρι *mesimeri* (n.) noon
μεσημεριανό *mesimeriano* (n.) lunch
μετά *meta* after
μεταλλικό νερό *metalliko nero* (n.) mineral water
μέτρα *metra* (n.) meters
μέτριο *metrio* medium
μηδέν *miTHen* zero
Μη καπνίζετε *Mi kapnizete* No Smoking
μήλο *milo* (n.) apple
μήνας *minas* (m.) month
μητέρα *mitera* (f.) mother
μηχανή *mihani* (f.) engine
μηχανικός *mihanikos* (m.) mechanic

VOCABULARY

μία *mia* a, an, one
μιλάω *milao* to speak
μιλάτε . . . *milate* Do you speak . . . ?
μονόκλινο *monoklino* single room
μονόδρομος *monoTHromos* (m.)
one-way traffic
μοσχάρι *moshari* (n.) beef
μοσχαράκι *mosharaki* (n.) veal
μουσικοχορευτικό *moosikohoreftiko* musical
μόνο *mono* only
μόνος *monos* alone
μουσείο *moosio* (n.) museum
μπακλαβάς *baklavas* (m.) baklava
μπάμιες *bamies* (f.) okra
μπάνιο *banio* (n.) bath
μπαρ *bar* (n.) bar
μπαρμπούνι *barbooni* (n.) red mullet
μπαταρία *bataria* (f.) battery
μπιζέλια *bizelia* (n.) peas
μπικίνι *bikini* (n.) bikini
μπισκότα *biskota* (n.) biscuits
μπλε *ble* blue
μπλούζα *blooza* (f.) blouse
Μπορώ να . . . *boro na* . . . May I . . .
μπριζόλες *brizoles* (f.) chops
μπουζούκι *boozooki* (n.) bouzouki
μπουκάλι *bookali* (n.) bottle
μπύρα *bira* (f.) beer

Ναι *ne* yes
ναός *naos* (m.) temple
ναυαγοσώστης *navagosostis* (m.)
lifeguard
ναυτία *naftia* (f.) sea sickness
νέα *nea* (n.) news
νερό *nero* (n.) water
νησί *nisi* (n.) island
νοσοκομείο *nosokomio* (n.) hospital
νοικιάζω *nikiazo* to rent, to hire
νομίζω *nomizo* to think
νόμισμα *nomisma* (n.) coin
ντήζελ *dizel* diesel
ντισκοτέκ *diskotek* (n.) discotheque
ντολμάδες *dolmaTHes* (m.) stuffed
vine leaves
ντομάτα *domata* (f.) tomato
ντομάτες γεμιστές *domates yemistes*
stuffed tomatos
ντοματόσουπα *domatosoopa* (f.)
tomato soup

ντοματοσαλάτα *domatosalata* (f.)
tomato salad
ντους *doosh* (n.) shower
νύχτα *nihta* (f.) night
νυχτερινό κέντρο *nihterino kendro* (n.)
night club

Ξανά *ksana* again
ξαφνικά *ksafnika* suddenly
ξεκινάω *ksekinao* to start off
ξεναγός *ksenagos* (m. f.) guide
Ξενοδοχείο *ksenoTHohio* (n.) hotel
ξέρω *ksero* I know
ξυφίας *ksifias* (m.) swordfish
ξυριστική μηχανή *ksiristiki mihani* (f.)
electric razor

Ογδόντα *ogTHonda* eighty
οδηγός *oTHigos* guide book, driver
οδηγείτε (οδηγώ) *othigite (othigo)* to
drive (I drive)
οδική κυκλοφορία *oTHiki kikloforia* (f.)
traffic
οδικός χάρτης *oTHikos hartis* (m.) road
map
οδοντόβουρτσα *oTHondovoortsa* (f.)
toothbrush
οδοντογιατρός *oTHontoyiatros* (m.)
dentist
οδοντόκρεμα *othondokrema* (f.)
toothpaste
οδός *oTHos* (f.) street
ομελέττα *omeletta* (f.) omelette
οικογένεια *ikoyenia* (f.) family
ομπρέλλα ηλίου *ombrella ilioo* (f.)
beach umbrella
όνομα *onoma* (n.) name
ορεκτικά *orektika* (n.) appetizers
ορίστε *oriste* here you are
όριο ταχύτητος *orio tahititas* (n.)
speed limit
όροφος *orofos* (m.) floor
ούζο *oozo* (n.) ouzo
όχι *ohi* no
οκτακόσια *oktakosia* eight hundred
οκτώ *okto* eight

Παγωμένος, η, ο *pagomenos, i, o*
iced, chilled
παιδάκια *paiTHakia* (n.) lamp chops
πάγκος *pagos* (m.) bench
παγωτό *pagoto* (n.) ice cream
παθαίνω *patheno* to suffer

VOCABULARY

παιδί *peTHi* (n.) child
παίρνω *perno* to take
πακέτο τσιγάρα *paketo tsigara* (n.) pack of cigarettes
παντελόνι *pandeloni* (n.) pants
παιχνίδι *pehniTHi* (n.) toy, game
παντρεμένος, η, ο *pandremenos, married*
παντού *pandoo* everywhere
παράδοση *paraTHosi* (f.) tradition
παρακαλώ *parakalo* please, don't mention it
παρέκαμψη *parakampsi* (f.) detour
παραλία *paralia* (f.) beach
Παρασκευή *Paraskevi* (f.) Friday
παράσταση *parastasi* (f.) performance
πάρκινγκ *parking* (n.) parking
πάρτε (παίρνω) *parte (perno)* to take (I take)
παρκόμετρο *parkometro* (n.) parking meter
πατάτες *patates* (f.) potatoes
πατάτες τηγανιτές *patates tiganites* (f.) french fries
πεζόδρομος *pezoTHromos* (m.) pedestrian zone
Πέμπτη *Pempti* (f.) Thursday
πενήντα *peninda* fifty
πεντακόσια *pendakosia* five hundred
πέντε *pende* five
πεπόνι *peponi* (n.) melon
περιμένω *perimeno* to wait for
περιοδεία *perioTHia* (f.) tour
περιοδικό *perioTHiko* (n.) magazine
περίπου *peripoo* about
περίπτερο *periptero* (n.) newsstand
περνάω ωραία *pernao orea* to have a good time
πέτρες *petres* (f.) stones
πετσέτα *petseta* (f.) towel
πηγαίνω *piyeno* to go
πηρούνι *pirooni* (n.) fork
πιάτο *piato* (n.) plate
πίεση *piesi* (f.) blood pressure
(να) πιούμε (πίνω) *na pioome (pino)* to drink (I drink)
πιπέρι *piperi* (n.) pepper
πιπεριές *piperies* (f.) peppers
πισίνα *pisina* (f.) swimming pool
πιστωτική κάρτα *pistotiki karta* (f.) credit card
πλαζ *plaz* (f.) beach
πλατεία *platia* (f.) square, stalls
πληροφορίες *plirofories* (f.) information
πλάτη *plati* (f.) back (anat.)
πλήρης ασφάλεια *pliris asfalia* full insurance

να πληρώσει (πληρώνω) *na plirosete (plirono)* to pay (I pay)
πλησιέστερος, η, ο *plisiesteros i, o* nearest
πλοίο *plio* (n.) ship
(με τα) πόδια *(me ta) poTHia* on foot
ποδήλατο θάλασσας *pothilato thalassas* (n.) pedal boat
ποιός, α, ο *pios, a, o*? who?
πνίγεται *pniyetai* she/he is drowning
πόλη *poli* (f.) city
πολύ *poli* very much
πολυθρόνα *polithrona* (f.) armchair
(με) πονάει *(me) ponai* it hurts
πονόδοντος *ponoTHondos* (m.) toothache
πονοκέφαλος *ponokefalos* (m.) headache
πόνος *ponos* (m.) pain
πόρτα *porta* (f.) door
πορτ-μπαγκάζ *port-bagaz* (n.) trunk (of car)
πορτοκαλάδα *portokalaTHa* (f.) orange
πορτοκάλι *portokali* (n.) orangeade
πόσιμο *posimo* drinkable
πόσο . . . ; *poso?* How much . . .?
πότε . . . ; *pote?* when . . .?
πόσα . . . ; *posa?* How many . . .?
ποτήρι *potiri* (n.) glass
ποτό *poto* (n.) drink
πουκάμισο *pookamiso* (n.) shirt
πούλμαν *poolman* (n.) coach
πουλόβερ *poolover* (n.) sweater/pullover
πούρο *pooro* (n.) cigar
πράσινο *prasino* green
πρατήριο βενζίνης *pratirio venzinis* (n.) gas station
πρεσβεία *presvia* (f.) embassy/consulate
πρησμένος *prismenos* swollen
προβλήματα *provlimata* (n.) problems
πρόγραμμα *programma* (n.) program
προκαταβολή *prokatavoli* (f.) deposit
προορισμός *proorismos* (m.) destination
πρόσκλιση *prosklisi* (f.) invitation
προσοχή *prosohi* caution, attention
πρωί *proi* (n.) morning
πρωινό *proino* (n.) breakfast
πτήση *ptisi* (f.) flight

πυρετός *piretos* (m.) fever
πυροσβέστης *pirosvestis* (m.)
  fireman
πυροσβεστική αντλία *pirosvestiki
  andlia* (f.) fire department

Ρέστα *resta* change
ρετσίνα *retsina* (f.) retsina
ροδάκινα *roтнakina* (n.) peaches
ρολόι *roloi* (n.) clock, watch
ρύζι *rizi (n.)* rice

Σάββατο *Savvato* Saturday
Σαββατοκύριακο *Savvatokyriako* (n.)
  weekend
σάλτσα *saltsa* (f.) sauce
σαμπουάν *sampooan* (n.) shampoo
σάντουιτς *sandooits* (n.) sandwich
σαπούνι *sapooni* (n.) soap
σαράντα *saranda* forty
σειρά *sira* turn
σερβιέτες υγείας *serviettes iyias*
  (f.) sanitary napkins
σημαδούρα *simaтнoora* (f.) buoy
σήμερα *simera* today
(πιό) σιγά *(ryo) siga* more slowly
σίγουρος, η, ο *sigooros, i, o* certain
σιδηρόδρομος *siтнiroтнromos* (m.)
  railway
σινεμά *sinema* (n.) cinema
σκέτος καφές *sketos kafes* coffee
  without sugar
σλάιντς *slaids* (n.) slides
σόδα *soтнa* (f.) soda
σοκολάτα *sokolata* (f.) chocolate
σουβλάκι *soovlaki* (n.) souvlaki
σούπα *soopa* (f.) soup
σούπερ βενζίνη *sooper venzini* (f.)
  super gas
σπασμένος *spasmenos* broken
σπίτι *spiti* (n.) house
σπουδάζω *spooтнazo* to study
σπρέι *sprei* (n.) spray
στάδιο *staтнio* (n.) stadium
σταθμός *stathmos* (m.) station
σταθμός ταξί *stathmos taxi* taxi
  stand
σταμάτησε (σταματάω) *stamatise
  (stamatao)* stop (I stop)
στάση *stasi* (f.) (bus) stop
σταφύλια *stafilia* (n.) grapes
στενό *steno* (n.) side street
στενός, η, ο *stenos* tight, narrow
στην υγεία σας *stin iyia sas*
  cheers!
στιγμή *stigmi* (f.) moment

στραμπούλιξα (στραμπουλίζω)
  stramboliksa, (stramboolizo) I
  sprained (I sprain)
στρίψτε (στρίβω) *stripste* (strivo)
  turn
στρώμα θάλασσας *stroma thalassas*
  air matress
στυλό *stilo* (n.) ballpoint pen
σύγκρουση *singroosi* (f.) collision
συγνώμη *signomi* sorry
σύκα *sika* (n.) figs
συμπληρώστε (συμπληρώνω)
  simbliroste (simblirono) fill in
  (I fill in)
συνάλλαγμα *sinallagma* (n.)
  currency exchange
συναυλία *sinavlia* (f.) concert
συννεφιά *sinnefia* (f.) cloudy
συνοδός *sinoтнos* (m.) guide
συνταγή *sindayi* (f.) prescription
συστημένο *sistimeno* registered
  letter
(να σας) συστηθώ *(na sas) sistitho*
  Let me introduce myself
συχνά *sihna* often

Ταβέρνα *taverna* (f.) taverna
ταμείο *tamio* (n.) cash desk
ταξίδι *taksiтнi* (n.) trip
ταραμοσαλάτα *taramosalata* (f.)
  fish roe salad
ταχυδρομείο *tahiтнromio* (n.) post
  office
ταχύτητα *tahitita* (f.) speed
τελειώνω *teliono* to finish
τελωνείο *telonio* (n.) customs
τέντα *tenda* (f.) tent
τηλεγράφημα *tilegrafima* (n.)
  telegram
τηλεφωνείστε (τηλεφωνώ) *tilefoniste*
  (tilefono) to telephone
  (I telephone)
τηλέφωνο *tilefono* (n.) telephone
τιμή *timi* (f.) price
τόστ *tost* (n.) toast
τουαλέττα *tooaletta* (f.) toilet
τουρίστας *tooristas* (m.) tourist
  (man)
Τουριστικός οδηγός *tooristikos
  oтнigos* (m.) tourist guide
Τουριστική Αστυνομία *tooristiki
  astinomia* (f.) tourist police
τουρίστρια *tooristria* (f.) tourist
  (woman)
τράπεζα *trapeza* (f.) bank
τροχόσπιτο *trohospito* (n.) trailer

VOCABULARY

τσιγάρο *tsigaro* (n.) cigarette
τσάι με γάλα *tsai me gala* (n.) tea
  with milk
τσάι με λεμόνι *tsai me lemoni* (n.)
  tea with lemon
τυρί *tyri* (n.) cheese
τυρόπιτα *tiropita* (f.) cheese pie

Υπάρχει *iparhi* there is
υπογραφή *ipografi* (f.) signature
υπογράψτε (υπογράφω) *ipograpste*
  (*ipografo*) to sign (I sign)
υπόσχεσαι (υπόσχομαι) *iposhese*
  (*iposhome*) do you promise?
  (I promise)
ύφασμα *ifasma* (n.) material, fabric

φάγαμε (τρώω) *fagame* (*tro-o*) we
  ate (I eat)
φαγητό/φαΐ *fagito*, (n.)/*fai* food
φάκελλος *fakellos* (m.) envelope
φανάρι *fanari* (n.) traffic lights
φαρμακείο *farmakio* (n.) pharmacy
φασολάκια φρέσκα *fasolakia freska*
  (n.) green beans
φεριμπότ *feribot* (n.) ferry boat
φέρνω *ferno* I bring
φέτα *feta* (f.) feta cheese
φέτος *fetos* this year
φεύγω *fevgo* I leave
φημισμένος, η, ο *fimismenos*
  famous
φιλοξενία *filoksenia* (f.) hospitality
φίλος, φίλη *filos* (m.), *fili* (f.) friend
φοιτητής *fititis* (m.) student (male)
φοιτήτρια *fititria* (f.) student
  (female)
φόρεμα *forema* (n.) dress
φόρος *foros* (m.) tax
φραντζόλα *frantzola* (f.) loaf of
  bread
φράουλες *fraooles* (f.) strawberries
φρέσκος *freskos* fresh
φρούτα *froota* (n.) fruit
φτάνω *ftano* I arrive
φτηνός *ftinos* cheap
φωτιά *fotia* (f.) fire

χαίρετε *herete* hello/goodbye
  (formal)
χαίρομαι *herome* I'm glad
χαίρω πολύ *hero poli* pleased to
  meet you
χάρτης *hartis* (m.) map
να χαλάσω (χαλάω) *na halaso*
  (*halao*) to change (I change)
  money
χάθηκε (χάνομαι) *hathike* (*hanome*)
  it got lost (I get lost)

χαρτί τουαλέττας *harti tooalettas*
  toilet paper
χαρτονόμισμα *hartonomisma* (m.)
  bill (money)
χθές *hthes* yesterday
χορός *horos* (m.) dance
χρειάζομαι *hriazome* I need
χρέωση *herosi* (f.) charge
να χρησιμοποιήσω *na hrisimopiiso*
  to use
χωριάτικη *horiatiki* traditional
  Greek salad
χωρίς *horis* without

Ψάρι *psari* (n.) fish
ψιλά *psila* (n.) change
ψωμί *psomi* (n.) bread

ωραίος, α, ο *oreos, a, o* nice
ώρα *ora* time (f.) hour